THE PYRAMID PUZZLE

THE PYRAMID PUZZLE

Igniting Transformation with the Power of Trust

a business story

ZAIN RAJ

THE PYRAMID PUZZLE
IGNITING TRANSFORMATION WITH THE POWER OF TRUST
By Zain Raj

First Edition

Published by
Munn Avenue Press
300 Main Street, Ste 21
Madison, NJ 07940
MunnAvenuePress.com

eBook ISBN # 978-1-960299-11-6
Paperback ISBN # 978-1-960299-07-9
Hardcover ISBN # 978-1-960299-08-6

Printed in the United States of America

Foreword/Invitation

There are many sad stories of once-great and once-storied *Fortune* 500 retail companies becoming shadows of their former selves and disappearing from public view. These were companies that employed thousands or tens of thousands of employees, were led by generations of families, and had scores of retail locations across America. These businesses were once so vital that they played a central role not only in our country's culture but in the lives of the families who regularly visited them to buy everything from food to clothing, to tires for cars, to technology devices for the home.

We grew up with these businesses and have memories attached to them. Racing around on new tricycles, buying the first suit for a job interview, scouring the aisles to find the perfect dress for prom, and staring at barbecue grills for the perfect backyard.

It's hard to believe that companies like these can fall behind the times, begin closing locations, and then vanish completely before our eyes. Sadly, the stories of the demise of these businesses are all too common in today's world.

But rarer still are the stories of companies who faced such adversity and found new, creative ways to turn things around and become relevant again—surviving and thriving past even the dreams of their founders decades ago.

This is a fictional story of a company that decided to fight to exist or die trying. The company in this novel has generations of battling heirs who had become too complacent in the company's long existence, expecting the good times to go on forever and the checks to keep rolling in, regardless of the creeping reality outside their front doors. What they didn't realize was how far the business had fallen into disrepair, how the once-proud retail locations had begun crumbling in plain sight, how the suppliers were becoming estranged, how the morale of management and employees at all levels reached historic lows, and how the customers, both brick and mortar and online, had been fleeing in great numbers for some time.

Why was this happening to a formerly respected and treasured enterprise? One word: trust. It had disappeared from the top, middle, and bottom of the company's business structure. But their customers felt it too. They felt it every time they dared visit a shabby, under-stocked retail location. In short, no one trusted each other: customers didn't trust anyone in the stores; suppliers didn't trust the merchants; workers didn't trust their managers; their managers didn't trust the management above them; and the strata of management above them didn't trust the C-suite and the Board of Directors.

The biggest, detrimental problem: When that trust erodes over time, it rarely can be restored, and a business that was profitable and successful for years and years dissolves into dust. Trust takes time to build up, but it's fragile and can be destroyed in an instant. Without trust, there is no confidence in the company or loyalty to it, and soon the optimistic possibilities of what it can achieve turn into distant, cynical pipe dreams.

But what would happen if a young, new CEO came into the

picture with a knowledgeable team, new thinking, and the energy and stamina to break the tide and right the ship? A fight between the old and new ways—and the older and younger heirs of the founder—would ensue for the company's very survival. Hard work, planning, and an aggressive strategy forward might just be the company's way out of the quagmire. This might even change the hardened, calcitrant minds and attitudes of even the most stubborn.

Overall, there are critical lessons to be gleaned from such a heroic journey if we're willing to listen and learn. When we create and nurture strong relationships, make valuable, emotional connections, and build trust throughout an enterprise, anything can—and does—happen.

Chapter One

Joseph Chandler felt that uncomfortable sixth sense that someone was staring at him.

A full professor at the University of Chicago Booth School of Business, he had only made tenure the year before. He was the youngest person to do so in the history of the school. Sitting in the nearby Plein Air Café, he even allowed himself to have one of their famous *pain au chocolat* to go with his coffee. He was about to head to the lecture hall to teach a class titled Business Failures and How to Avoid Them when he looked up from his notes and saw a well-dressed man with pale skin and blonde hair peering over his shoulder. "May I help you?" he asked guardedly.

He didn't assume this was going to be a confrontation but being Black and growing up in one of the toughest parts of Chicago (although he, himself, would never tell you that,) gave him a certain suspicion of anyone crowding him.

The stranger, who looked to be in his mid to late thirties, took a step back.

"I'm so sorry," he said, his tone sincere. "I just happened to be walking by and saw the Pyramid logo in your notes."

The bright blue script "P" with the famous slogan, "Pyramid!

50 Years of Giving the American People What They Want! Quality at a Great Price!" was featured on the first page of Joseph's notes.

Joseph chuckled. "Don't tell me... it brings back happy memories just seeing it?"

"Something like that," the stranger replied, smiling.

Joseph straightened out his papers. "I'm guessing you haven't shopped there lately."

"Actually, no," he admitted.

"You and everybody else," Joseph said, laughing. "Which is why I'm spending the next two hours discussing it with my students."

The young man smiled. "Oh, you're a professor at the B school! So ... why teach about Pyramid?"

"Well," Joseph said, sighing. "They went from being one of the great American success stories over the past fifty years to being on life support. So, I'm talking to my students about all the mistakes that were made along the way."

The stranger seemed genuinely interested. "Like what?"

"Well, to start with, they've let the business run into the ground by stubbornly sticking with the formula set up by their founder, old "Trader Larry" McCormack, rather than changing and adapting with the times," Joseph said. "Not to mention a Board of Directors made up of family members—typically a recipe for infighting and disaster that doesn't reward forward thinking."

The stranger ran his fingers through his hair. "So ... you think it's a basket case?"

"Hey, anything can happen, but it doesn't look good," Joseph said. "If I were you, I'd make a visit soon, because it might not be there if you wait too long."

The stranger nodded. "You know, they had the Fox Business

Channel on at the gym, and I noticed they've just hired a new CEO."

Joseph laughed. "Oh really? Well, good luck to that poor bastard. He's walking into a hornet's nest."

Joseph gathered his things. "Hey, nice talking to you."

"You, too," said the stranger.

Joseph stuck out his hand. "Joseph Chandler, pleased to meet you."

The young man shook his hand. "Skip Collinsworth. I'm the poor bastard who has taken the job as the new CEO of Pyramid."

Joseph stared at Skip for a moment, trying to regain his composure. "I ... see," he stuttered, embarrassed. "Well, I guess that'll teach me not to shoot off my big mouth before finding out who I'm talking to."

"Hey, I can't argue with you about what you said about Pyramid," Skip said. "Especially since I've been talking to investors and analysts around Chicago recently. I was taking a break. I went to the University of Chicago for undergrad. My old stomping grounds. This was my calm before the storm."

Joseph held the door for Skip as the two men headed out. "Maybe we can continue this after my class? I feel awful after saying all those things."

"You know what?" Skip said as he walked Joseph over to the broad steps leading to the impressive glass and concrete facade of the Charles M. Harper Center, in the heart of the Chicago campus. "You could do me an even bigger favor. Let me sit in on your class and hear what your young hotshots have to say. Maybe one of them can come up with something."

Joseph shrugged. "Sure," he replied, studying Skip. "If you don't mind hearing some more hard truths. My students are probably ready to tear your poor company apart."

"I can take it," Skip smiled, and the two men headed off to Joseph's class.

Chapter Two

As Joseph and Skip walked into the great vaulted lobby of the Harper Center's Rothman Winter Garden with the sun streaming through its steel Gothic arches, Skip paused to take in the scene. Students were rushing by to get to their classes as faculty members greeted one another.

"I can't imagine they'll say anything I haven't thought of myself," Skip said as the two men headed to Room C10, home to Joseph's class. Today the discussion would be focused on the once-great brand that has fallen by the wayside.

"They're bright kids," Joseph said. "They might just surprise you. They always surprise me."

They entered and Skip took a seat in the back of the large lecture hall. He watched as the throngs of students filed into the classroom, chatting amongst themselves. It brought him back to his days at B school in Cambridge, Massachusetts. Harvard Business School was a little stuffier than this, with a few more hard elbows and a certain New England reserve.

In those days, if anyone had told him that he would, one day, head up one of the most storied retail businesses in the country, he'd have laughed in that person's face. But here he was.

At the podium, Joseph Chandler cleared his throat and spoke

with a quiet, professorial authority into the microphone. "Okay, everyone, let's settle down."

The room immediately went silent.

"Now," began Joseph as the first slide went up. "Can anyone tell me who this is?"

It was a photo from the 70s of a red-faced man in a baseball cap, with his arm hanging out of a beat-up Chevrolet Suburban.

Every hand went up.

Joseph laughed, "Okay, does anyone *not* know who this is? Of course, it's "Trader Larry" McCormack in his trademark, twelve-year-old Chevy truck. You all know the legend—even when his company was worth billions, he insisted on driving around in that old thing. No limos, no town cars, no drivers for Trader Larry. Am I right?"

The class murmured their surprise that a captain of industry like Trader Larry wouldn't avail himself of every possible perk. They certainly would, given a chance.

The next slide showed Trader Larry cutting the ribbon in front of a new Pyramid store, circa 1980. Everyone around him —executives, workers, customers—looked thrilled to be part of this American story.

Joseph looked up at the photo above him.

"Don't let that aw-shucks expression fool you," he told his students. "Even when I was in B school, we studied how Trader Larry very aggressively built his company, one store at a time, city after city, state by state, until his brand was synonymous with retail success."

He looked out at his students with a small smile.

"Maybe it wasn't the upscale success of Gucci or other luxury brands. But that wasn't the McCormack way. His goal was simple: Give American-made products to the working man at a low price and a great value."

A student in the middle of the room raised her hand. Joseph pointed in her direction.

"But he still made huge profits, right? I mean, wasn't he one of the wealthiest men in the country?" she asked.

He nodded and looked back up at the screen, where the genial Trader Larry was shaking hands with some of his customers.

"Look at him in that worn-out synthetic suit," he continued. "It probably went back to his days as a traveling salesman. That's exactly what endeared him to the millions of lower-income citizens, who could look at ol' Larry and think, 'He's just like me! He shares my values of hard work and honest pay.' But don't let that fool you."

Professor Chandler turned back to his students with a look of warning. "He was a very astute businessman and looked for every opportunity to find new ways to keep his prices lower than the competition."

Another slide went up, this one of an office complex from about the same era as McCormack's car and wardrobe.

"I guess the nicest way of saying this is that Larry McCormack stayed frugal, no matter how much he had. He built his modest corporate headquarters in the South Side of Chicago, happily running his business empire from there. His vendors found themselves sitting on a Pyramid recliner instead of a fancy chair. And the buyer they were meeting with was sitting at an old, banged-up desk that you wouldn't have in your own office today for all the tea in China."

Another hand went up. This time it was a bearded, young man with an intense expression on his face. "Professor Chandler?"

Chandler nodded at him.

The student had a slight European accent. "How did he keep his prices so low?"

Joseph brightened. "Good question! His merchants depended on his huge orders, so he called the tune. And if they couldn't match his price, he would simply buy from someone who could."

The bearded student nodded. "Excuse me, please. What if that 'someone' had moved their factories offshore?"

"So be it," Joseph answered. "His customers didn't care. They saw American flags in every store, friendly neighbors welcoming them in, and every type of product for all their needs, at better prices than they could get anywhere else. The guests loved their Pyramid."

Skip sat back in his seat and sighed. *The stock market liked what it saw as well back then, as profit margins moved skyward. Those were the golden years, all right,* he thought to himself.

A tall, striking girl with blonde hair in the second row raised her hand. Joseph perked up.

"Yes, Gabby?"

"So, when did things change?" she asked.

Joseph moved on to the next slide. It had a graph on it. "When old Trader Larry was found dead in his Suburban, at the age of 86, on the side of an Interstate, having lived the American dream."

The class, transfixed, studied the graph, which depicted profit curves for Pyramid and a few of its competitors. It showed that Trader Larry's company was already heading along a definite downward curve.

"Mind you," Joseph explained. "By that time, Pyramid was already squeezed. Other retailers had picked up on his tricks and were using them to lure customers into their megastores with more upscale products."

"Change was needed as the stock was heading downward. But that's hard to do when you've got managers stuck in the past and a Board consisting of Larry McCormack's children and grandchildren who didn't want to rock the boat."

Joseph looked around the lecture hall at some of the brightest minds in business schools anywhere in the nation.

"So," he said, clapping his hands. "Any ideas of how to help this company find its footing before it goes bye-bye?"

A burly kid, who Skip sized up to be a former college football player, raised his hand. "Look, if the managers aren't going to change—change the managers. Right?"

Joseph raised his eyebrows and smiled. "Okay, let's talk about that. I mean, you want the best you can get, right?"

"Of course," said the young man.

Joseph flipped back in the slides on his laptop to the picture of the Pyramid corporate headquarters. "So, that means working out of the company's offices in Chicago's South Side, where land is cheap and the neighborhoods are dicier than the West Loop, Gold Coast, or the city's North Side. It's not a pleasant place to visit. But convince a first-class manager to work there full-time? Would you want to be there?"

"Maybe," the young man said, none too convincingly. The young man turned visibly red.

"Look, it's nothing to be ashamed of," Joseph told them. "Why would you want to spend every day in Fuller Park when you could be drinking lattes and using the climbing wall at your cool new office in Silicon Valley, hipster Brooklyn, or in trendy River North Chicago?"

Murmurs of assent filled the hall.

In the back row, none of this was news to Skip. He'd lost track of all the lunches he'd spent trying to convince some recruits to come to help him right the ship. The few he could convince to work for Pyramid all wanted to work remotely. Many said, "No, thanks."

The conversation about what was wrong with Pyramid and how hard it would be for anyone to turn around the company continued as more and more students asked questions of the professor or offered solutions, none of which seemed easy or even remotely applicable. Pyramid might not be a complete failure yet, but from the way the discussion was going, it was only a matter of time.

Then another young man stood up. He looked uncomfortable and was dressed in a pair of wrinkled chinos and a worn sweater. He spoke with a noticeable Southern accent. "Professor, I need to say something," the young man said.

Joseph checked his seating chart. This young man hadn't said anything all semester. "Go ahead, um, Silas."

Silas put his hands in his pockets. "It's just that, well, we've been talking about these various businesses like they were just bugs under a microscope or something. Pyramid is a lot more than that to me. My family shopped there for as long as I can remember."

Silas looked around the room. "Am I the only one here who actually shopped at Pyramid? Who knows what it once meant to us?"

There was an uncomfortable silence.

Then, from the front of the room: "No," Joseph said. "You're not the only one. I did, too. Once upon a time."

Skip sat up straight in his chair when he heard that. Joseph noticed. He checked his watch. It was nearing the end of class.

"So," he said, turning once again to the room at large, and catching Skip's eye. "Let's say the brand-new CEO of Pyramid was here in the room with us right now. What would you tell him?"

Silence.

Then the ex-jock piped up. "Quit! Get out while you can!"

There was general laughter and applause in the room. The bell rang.

"That's it for today," Joseph called out as the students packed up their laptops, grabbed their backpacks, and headed out.

Skip, who had been paying avid attention, slumped back in his chair. It had been a brutal two hours. Between Joseph's analysis and the questions and comments the students had made, he felt worse than ever about Pyramid's future. *Was there any way to get this company back on track?* he thought.

The only bright spot had been the tall girl with blonde hair. She seemed to always have the most cogent answers and kept steering the conversation back to the customers and how to bring them back. It was as if she really cared about making things better, not just winning some academic argument.

Skip made his way down to the podium, where Joseph was gathering his things.

"You look a little pale," Joseph remarked. "Even for a White guy."

Skip gave a dry laugh. "Yeah, well, a two-hour pounding will do that to you."

"Hey, it wasn't all bad," Joseph said. "I think there were some good ideas there."

"Can we talk for a moment?" Skip asked.

"Sure," Joseph said. "I've got office hours right now, but we can definitely keep talking."

"That would be great," Skip said. "I thought coming back to campus would be the calm before the storm. I guess it just showed me that the storm's even bigger than I thought."

The two men headed out of the seminar room and down the corridor toward Joseph's office.

Chapter Three

After a short walk, they reached an office with a sign that read, "Professor Chandler, Office Hours M/W/TH 2-4 p.m."

"I'm so glad you came," Joseph said. "They're a tough crowd, I admit."

"Listen," Skip said. "They actually raised some really good questions. Can we talk about what they said?"

Joseph gestured to a student sitting in a chair next to his office. "You'll have to ask her. She's got an appointment with me."

Skip looked down and saw it was the tall, blonde girl Joseph had referred to as Gabby.

She peered at him for a second. "Weren't you the guy who was sitting in the back of the lecture? I noticed you didn't seem to be having too good a time."

Joseph laughed. "Where are my manners? Gabrielle Richardson, this is Skip Collinsworth, the new CEO of Pyramid Stores."

Gabby's eyes widened. "Oh, er, well ... in that case ... no wonder."

"I liked what you had to say in there," Skip said. "You

seemed to be the only one concerned with the people we're supposed to be selling to."

Gabby shrugged. "Hey, it's the ex-sociology major in me. We're the ones who are always curious about how things affect people and society at large. I'm always looking for the human element."

"You're a sociologist?" Skip asked.

"Well, I *was,*" Gabby replied. "Until I took an Intro to Business course as an undergrad from this visiting professor named Joseph Chandler. Turned my whole life around. I became a business major right then and there. I mean, it was either business or professional sports, and I was kind of done with that."

Gabrielle Richardson. The name sounded so familiar to Skip. Then it hit him. "Wait a minute!" he said. "You're *that* Gabrielle Richardson! You won the silver medal at the Olympics, right? You were all over the news!"

Joseph winced.

Gabrielle's face turned an interesting shade of red. "Yes, well. I don't like to—"

"I mean, you came *this close* to winning the gold. That's pretty impressive," said Skip.

Gabby was gritting her teeth. "That's *very kind of you,*" she said.

Skip looked confused. "I'm sorry, is this a sore subject? You did win the silver medal, and that's pretty good—"

"Silver isn't gold," Gabby said curtly. She sat back down. "Go ahead and have your meeting. I've got time."

"Thanks," said Skip and followed Joseph into his office.

Skip immediately noticed that Joseph's office was as put together as he was, with papers in neatly labeled folders on his desk and books arranged on his bookshelf, perfectly lined up.

This is a man who doesn't like chaos, Skip thought.

Joseph put his papers from the lecture in front of him on the desk.

"So, what was that all about?" Skip asked.

Joseph grinned. "Oh, Gabby. Yeah, she's a little touchy about that medal thing."

"But she came *this close* to winning the heptathlon!" Skip exclaimed. "That's the hardest event of the entire Olympics. I ran track in college, and I follow the sport avidly."

"The operative phrase here is '*this close,*'" Joseph told him. "She lost her concentration at the very last second of the 800 meters."

"Wasn't there a whole thing about the Danish girl? I forget her name—jostling her?" asked Skip.

Joseph put on his reading glasses. "Gabby doesn't make excuses. And she *hates* to lose. She was the best athlete at New Trier and led her college basketball team to three championships. Then she was a star athlete as an undergrad, and she went to the Olympics."

"Wow, she's quite a world beater," Skip said.

Joseph looked up from his notes. "You're no slouch yourself. I read that you graduated from the University of Chicago summa cum laude and have degrees from both Harvard Law School and Harvard Business School. So, why aren't you a high-flying consultant instead of a CEO of a failing company?"

"Funny story," said Skip. "I was at one time. For a while, I was the golden boy at McKinsey and Company, 'destined for greatness.'"

Joseph sat back in his chair. "So, what happened?"

"Let's just say that a decade of flying on scheduled flights with strangers and staying in Marriotts and Hiltons started to get old," Skip replied. "So, I decided it was time to create a small consulting company of my own. And on my way out, as a parting gift to myself, I took a few of the firm's military clients with me."

Joseph blanched. "Let me guess. They weren't just going to sit there and let you walk off with their toys."

Skip nodded. "You know what Ralph Waldo Emerson said: 'Never strike a king unless you are sure to kill him.'"

"So, they laid down the law?" Joseph asked.

Skip looked out the window. "Nothing was said or done explicitly. Just a few vague threats to my clients of reaching out to superiors and limiting the success of their military careers if they did not comply."

"And just like that, you became a consultant with no clients."

Skip sighed. "Something like that."

"That still doesn't answer the question," said Joseph. "What brought you to Pyramid?"

"So, this college buddy of mine's wife had gone to Smith with Jenna McCormack," Skip began.

Joseph tried not to smile. He saw where this was going. "So, you married a McCormack, huh?" he asked, referring to one of the many offspring of Trader Larry, who spent money like there was no tomorrow and was keenly focused on the price of Pyramid stock.

"She's not a typical McCormack," Skip replied. "If you know what I mean. And at first, after we married, I was just going to consult, you know?"

"Uh-huh," Joseph answered, not very convincingly.

"Really!" Skip insisted. "Jenna felt that the family business desperately needed some new eyes and fresh thinking. Sure, Jen is an heiress to the McCormack fortune, but she has become frustrated by what the family business has become. She genuinely cares about its legacy."

Joseph raised his eyebrows. "A *caring* McCormack? *Really?*"

Like many in the business world, Joseph had heard about the supposed reputations of the McCormack children and their heirs. Far from driving around in beat-up Chevrolet Suburbans, the grandchildren of Trader Larry were famous for living lives unimaginable to the people who shopped at Pyramid stores across the Midwest.

"So, she proposed to the Board that I run the company," Skip said.

"How did that go over?" Joseph asked. "I thought a McCormack had always run the family business. I mean, they were running it into the ground, but they were still running it. How did she convince them to turn over the reins?"

Skip took a breath. "Have you seen the stock price lately? They love Trader Larry and the Pyramid legacy, but they love money more if I can be frank. Basically, no one else wanted the job."

"And if the company goes down, you're the fall guy," said Joseph.

"Exactly," answered Skip. "But I'm going to make sure it doesn't."

Joseph held up his hand. "Why is this so important to you?"

Skip got up and faced the window. He paused. Then he finally said, "I don't know… maybe I need to prove that I can do it. And maybe because I love my wife. We just had a baby and named her Carrie. I want her to grow up in a family business that she can have pride in… at least, someday." He then turned to Joseph. "I mean, that's why I wanted to talk right now. You asked a lot of good questions in that class. How about answers? Do you have any of those?"

Joseph thought for a moment. He had been looking for a new challenge. Was this what he'd been searching for?

"You know…" Joseph began, and then his voice trailed off.

"Go ahead," Skip said, cautiously.

Joseph cleared his throat. "Actually, I think I could help you," he said carefully. He realized he had a sabbatical coming up that he could take. He had been pondering which project he should focus on. Perhaps this was....

"But I'm not looking for any ivory tower advice," Skip quickly said. "I don't know that I have time to experiment. Do you realize what a short leash I'm on? I've probably got nine months max to get things turned around."

"I was a consultant and in business for ten years before I came back to academics," Joseph replied. "Everything I teach is drawn from my real-world experiences. I share lessons that I have learned from helping clients solve difficult problems across different categories. I think I can bring a fresh perspective to your problems."

"The *last* thing I need is another consultant," Skip countered. "You want consultants? I've got a whole floor of them. One of each flavor. McKinsey, BCG, Bain..."

"Those are some pretty heavy hitters," Joseph admitted. "Why is it that *they* haven't come up with solutions?"

Skip turned back to face Joseph. "Look, so we've both been consultants. You know the problem. They all have their approved methodologies and have provided a long list of recommendations. My leadership team has been championing some of these ideas, but they require a huge investment and a long-term horizon to see any meaningful impact. And some of their tactical ideas are just hard to execute at scale in the time I have."

Joseph thought of all his case studies. It seemed simple. "If they're not pulling their weight—"

"Don't you think I've tried to get rid of them?" Skip said, shaking his head. "They're so deeply entrenched in our corporate culture that even though I'm the CEO, I couldn't dislodge them with a crowbar. You'll excuse me if I take a dim view of consultants. There are many good ones. You were probably one of them. But you have to admit, most of them are more concerned with billing their hours and moving to the next project. I tried to be a different kind of consultant, but that's not the path I was supposed to go down, I suppose."

Joseph sat silent for a moment. "You asked me for answers. I'll need to see everything that's gone wrong before I can help you." He looked Skip straight in the eye. "And you do need help."

Skip nodded. "I tell you what. Come down to the headquarters and see what you think. If you feel you can get me out of this hole, I'm all for it."

The men shook hands.

Joseph checked his watch. "Wow. That was some small chat. Poor Gabby's been waiting out there for almost an hour."

He opened the door. Gabby was pounding away on her laptop. She looked up.

"I'm so sorry I took up your professor's time," Skip said. "I really appreciate it."

Gabby looked up from her screen. "What? Oh, that's fine."

Skip looked curiously at what had kept her undivided attention. "Oh! You do crossword puzzles? I used to do those when I was back at Harvard."

Gabby held up the page. "These are a little different." The title read, 'Cryptic Crossword.'

Skip looked at the clues. They seemed to be gibberish. '*Some forget to get here for gathering.*' What does that even mean?"

"You've got to figure out what type of clue it is, then what the definition is, and then how to solve it," Gabby explained. "For example, I guessed that 'gathering' was the clue and that the answer was hidden in the other words—'forGET TO GET HERe.' *Get-together* is a gathering. See?"

Skip shook his head. "Wow. That's amazing. How did you learn how to do that?"

Gabby smiled. "I had a good teacher."

Chapter Four

Skip shook hands with Joseph once more. "See you in Fuller Park." He smiled at Gabby. "Listen to this guy. He knows his stuff."

"You don't have to tell me that!" Gabby exclaimed, smiling, as Skip headed down the corridor to the elevator bank.

Joseph motioned her into the office. "Shall we?" he asked.

Gabby walked in and threw herself on the chair across from Joseph's desk. "So, Coach, are you literally helping that guy out?"

Joseph sat down and adjusted the file in front of him. Ever since he'd talked her into business school, Gabby had called him "Coach," but only in private. "Thinking about it, yes."

Gabby nodded. "Sounds like you're the guy to solve this."

"You think?" Joseph asked. "Listen, I want you to put on your social scientist's hat for a minute."

Gabby laughed. "I'm not sure it still fits. Maybe my head's gotten too big from all the statistics I've had to cram into it."

"I'm serious," Joseph said. "So, what do you make of Mr. Collinsworth?"

Gabby rubbed her chin with the back of her hand. She

reminded Joseph of a little kid who was given a hard math problem by the teacher.

"Well, other than being a grown man who still goes by the name 'Skip,' I think he seems like a good guy."

Joseph leaned back in his chair. "Seems?"

"He clearly comes from money. Probably never spoke to anyone outside of his class other than the help, even at Harvard. I grew up with guys like that. Maybe that's why I never went East for college."

Joseph refrained from pointing out that he wasn't from the same social class as Gabby and Skip. "So, he would need help in understanding the best way to communicate with people other than his social rank?"

"I would think so," Gabby said.

Joseph looked at her, grinning.

"Wait, are you suggesting I come with you to the headquarters?" Gabby asked.

Joseph got up and put on his jacket. "I don't think I'll be able to read all those boring reports myself! Are you up for taking a trip to the southern suburbs? Think I'm about to start my sabbatical."

"Okay, right behind you, Coach!" she exclaimed. "Lead the way!"

Chapter Five

Two days later, Joseph and Gabby made their way into the CEO's office at Pyramid headquarters in Fuller Park. The area south of Comiskey Park, now called Guaranteed Rate Field, is home to the White Sox. It was originally named after Melville Fuller, an Illinois native and former Chief Justice of the Supreme Court. And more recently, it served as the corporate home of Pyramid Stores.

"So," Gabby said, looking around, surprised. "I've never been in a CEO's office before. Do they all have shag carpeting?"

Joseph smiled. "Not even in the 70s. I think Trader Larry had, shall we say, a *unique* approach to decorating."

Gabby wrinkled her nose. "I can't place that smell. It's like..."

"To me, it smells like old Cup-a-Soup containers and desperation," Skip said, from behind the giant desk they were approaching. "I've tried everything to get rid of it, but it keeps coming back."

"Maybe you need an exorcism," suggested Gabby.

Skip gestured to the array of folders and stapled reports fanned out across his desk. "Well, Professor, this is your homework. You asked for all the historical reports, and here they are. On top is some of the stuff we've had to fight against as well."

Joseph sighed. "I guess we should get to work."

Gabby swept up half the folders. "I call dibs on the recliner!"

She settled into an ancient red La-Z-Boy and began to read.

Joseph looked at the top of the pile and winced. "Oh, yeah. I forgot about this."

A few years ago, one of the competing chain stores that was already gobbling up Pyramid's market share hired a Washington D.C. opposition research firm. This was a group that was paid to find dirt on presidential candidates. At the time, they were given the mission of turning up information about conditions in overseas factories from which Pyramid sourced many of its goods.

The resulting reports, which all the network and internet news outlets happily pounced on, showed surreptitious footage of children as young as eight or ten locked in factories in developing countries for eight to ten hours a day, sewing shirts for children their own age. This child prison labor turned out to account for a not-insignificant portion of the foreign goods that Pyramid imported.

Joseph read the attached report from a high-priced consultant who had been brought in because he was supposed to be well-versed in politics. His "brilliant" advice: "Just ignore the story and it will go away."

Skip saw Joseph reading the report. "I'm told that when he handed in his bill he said, 'They'll get bored within days and chase the next shiny object. I guarantee it.'" said Skip, sighing.

"And?" Joseph asked, already knowing the answer.

"Pyramid's failures to monitor working conditions in overseas factories dominated the news cycle for *ten full days*. Hey, we're 'America's favorite store.' Or we used to be, anyway. Of course, the story wouldn't die. "

In the folder were clippings and printouts of tweets. Headlines like "Does Slave Labor Build Pyramids?" and hashtags like #PyramidPrisonLabor flooded traditional and social media channels, prompting temporary boycotts of some Pyramid locations.

"I guess it couldn't get any worse!" Gabby exclaimed.

"Oh, yes it could," Skip said grimly. "Once reporters smell blood, they go in for the kill. A *New York Times* correspondent discovered that Pyramid employees were often no happier than Pyramid customers."

Joseph read from the article: "Pyramid has become, under Rockwell McCormack..."

"He was one of the worst leaders ever," Skip interjected. "I think he lasted nine months before he got bored and resigned."

Joseph nodded and continued: "'notorious for shifting the hours of workers at will, moving people from day to night shifts without regard for their personal lives."

Skip shook his head. "If you want to see it," he began. "I've got tons of video of salt-of-the-earth folks who worked at the stores telling their stories on local news outlets of how management was making it all but impossible for them to get their kids to school, take older relatives to healthcare appointments, or simply allow people to live normal lives. As you can imagine, the trust between workers and management was breaking down. And to make it worse, when the employees didn't like the hours they were given, they were fired."

Joseph reached for another folder. He turned to Skip. "And these, I hope, are the reports from those consultants on the floor downstairs? The ones with all the answers?"

Skip nodded. "Have at it."

A few hours into the process, Joseph looked up from the

tenth report he and Gabby had pored through. He shook his head and did an exasperated eye roll.

"That's what I was thinking," Gabby said. "Like this one, for example, is good at creating new accounting systems, which is important enough, but that's all they address. No one's looking at the big picture."

"Right," Joseph added, picking up random folders. "This one spent months installing new tracking software to monitor the sales of various SKUs across the company. And this one spent hundreds of thousands of dollars identifying geographic areas where the company could expand."

"But does a failing company have any business expanding until it gets its current house in order?" asked Gabby.

Joseph nodded. "I see a lot of different recommendations across many many different operating areas. What I don't see is anyone looking at the problems from a holistic, human-centered view. What is the real problem that Pyramid needs to address? Identifying that should be the critical priority to inform changes that can turn this ship around."

"Once again, professor, you've identified the problem," Skip said. "Now all you need to do is find me the solution."

Joseph sighed. "That's the hard part. Give me a bit of time to synthesize all the learning and come back to you with an answer."

"If you can come up with something," Skip said, his tone frank. "I'd be thrilled. I'm at my wit's end."

"Maybe we can," Joseph said. "No promises, but we'll do our best." He motioned to Gabby. "Let's go."

"Aw, I was just getting comfy," Gabby said, reluctantly leaving her recliner. She turned to Skip and said, "You should sell these in the store. People love recliners."

"If I could find a manufacturer who could make them that

well at a price where we could make a profit, I would," Skip said. "Story of my life right now."

Joseph led Gabby to the door. "I need to get out of here," he told her once they took their leave. "If I have to stare at that lime green carpet anymore, I'm going to get a migraine."

Gabby laughed, as they left the CEO suite, such as it was, to go back to Joseph's car for the ride back home. Could they really come up with an idea to turn Pyramid around?

Could anyone?

Chapter Six

The ride back thankfully had little traffic, and Joseph was able to drop Gabby off at her apartment by three in the afternoon.

"Listen, I'd like to thank you," Joseph said. "Let's have dinner next week. I want to talk through what we saw down there. If there's an answer for Pyramid, we'll solve it together."

"Um, sure," Gabby replied, surprised. "But would it be okay if my boyfriend came along?"

"Gabby, if you were thinking there was anything behind this invitation other than… I mean, I'm a happily married man, and I would never—"

Gabby laughed. "Relax, Coach. It's nothing like that. I just really like this guy, and I'd love for you two to meet, that's all."

"Of course! He's more than welcome!" Joseph said, relieved. "The Signature Room, eight o'clock?"

Gabby gave a thumbs-up and opened the door and walked away.

Joseph looked after her and wondered to himself, "What kind of man could win the heart of Gabrielle Richardson?"

• • •

In the Uber heading down North Michigan Avenue, Gabby's boyfriend, Sam, sat uncomfortably next to her. He tugged at his tie, which he very rarely wore.

"You look fine," Gabby assured him, patting his arm. "Stop fidgeting."

"I feel like I am back in high school, so dressed up," Sam said. For Sam, high school was a long way away. He had grown up in a small town in India. His prowess with Sanskrit texts and the epic poem Mahabharata had led to scholarships, first from the University of Mumbai for his undergraduate degree and then from the University of Chicago, where he was all but a dissertation away from his PhD in Ancient Indian Literature. He and Gabby had connected over their love of cryptic crosswords, which Sam, short for Samesh, did every week when they appeared in *The Times of India*.

"You should wear ties more often," Gabby said, squeezing his hand. "You look great."

Sam looked out the window at the city he'd learned to love, with its wide streets and bright lights at night. "I don't even know why I'm here. I don't know the first thing about business."

"First of all, Joseph insisted you join us," Gabby told him. "I think he feels like he wants to make sure he approves of you."

"Oh, that makes me feel better!" said the young man.

Gabby laid her head on his shoulder. "Anyway, how often do we get to go to one of Chicago's most exclusive and expensive restaurants?"

"Well, since I'm on a graduate student's stipend, don't get too used to it," he said.

"I promise!" Gabby smiled.

The car pulled up to the swanky lobby of the former John Hancock building. Their footsteps echoed on the expansive white marble floors leading to the elevators that would whisk them up to the ninety-fifth floor. Sam felt his stomach drop as they ascended.

Gabby bent down and whispered in his ear. "The real reason I want you here is that this business problem is a real puzzle. And you're so good at puzzles, right?"

The doors opened and even Gabby was taken aback by what greeted them—a 360-degree panorama of all of Chicago spread out around them, with tables brimming with well-dressed patrons speaking in hushed tones.

A gentleman in a vest and starched white shirt addressed Sam. "Good evening, sir. Do you have a reservation?"

The young man blanched. "Er ... I'm with her."

"Very good," the man said and turned to Gabby. "What name is the reservation under?"

"Chandler?" she said, guessing.

The man checked the book. "Yes, I see the rest of your party is already here. Please come this way."

Sam and Gabby followed him as he weaved through the tables of heavy hitters and elites who seemed so at home there. Joseph was looking at his phone as they arrived at the table and leapt to his feet.

"Gabby! You clean up nice."

Gabby looked down. "It's fun to put on grown-up clothes now and then."

Joseph turned toward Sam. "And this is...?"

The serious young man shook Joseph's hand, as Gabby introduced him. "Professor Joseph Chandler, Samesh Bhati, a doctoral candidate in Ancient Indian Studies."

"Nice to meet you." Joseph gestured to them to sit down. As the three of them perused the menu, he couldn't help but wonder, *How did these two meet?* "I've had both the swordfish and the lamb, and they're both delicious," Joseph suggested, as his two young guests surveyed The Signature Room's menu.

Sam was relieved to see the vegetarian options, all of which looked equally as good.

Since Joseph insisted on no business talk until after the main meal, they talked instead about Sam's journey to the States, how Joseph had worked for Obama's first political campaign, and they stayed away from discussing the Olympics.

Finally, the coffee arrived, and Gabby and Sam shared a chocolate mousse cake.

"I hope this business talk won't bore you," Joseph told Sam.

Sam put down his forkful of cake. "Not at all. It's all Gabby's been talking about since you guys went to Fuller Park."

Joseph sat back in his chair. "You have to understand. Unlike you two, I used to shop at Pyramid when I was a kid. In my head, I keep coming back, again and again, to the people who work there, and the people who shop there."

"And the people who *used* to shop and work there before the business took a turn for the worse," Gabby added.

Joseph leaned forward. "Exactly. The problem is not about selection, marketing campaigns, supply chain, or product mix. It's about more than that."

"They have done a lot of transactional and operational analyses," Gabby said. "But I didn't see much about their customers. They seem to be very light on true consumer insights."

"That's a great observation," Joseph told her. "I've seen it so many times. There are many discrete pieces of work without an overarching framework. They should have an integrated learning agenda that is focused on finding the fundamental problem to solve."

The conversation continued along this line, with ideas thrown out and debated.

As Sam listened, for the first time he began to understand what it was about the business that drew his girlfriend to it. Not abstract numbers, not just figures on a page, but working to make a difference in people's lives just as the Sanskrit texts he studied weren't only repositories of dead knowledge but living truths that still matter today.

"Look, the No. 1 issue seems to be this: how do we increase trust between all the stakeholders?" Joseph asked.

"Everyone in a company is your family," Sam said suddenly, and both Joseph and Gabby were surprised and turned to hear what the Sanskrit scholar had to say. "Everyone is connected. You have to take everyone together and consider everyone the same— customers, suppliers, and workers. This is where the Sanskrit phrase, *Vasudhaiva Kutumbakam* comes into the picture. It means, 'The world is one family.'"

Joseph looked at him, surprised. "Where did *that* come from?"

"The Mahabharata, actually," said Sam, shyly.

"It's great advice," Joseph said, approvingly. "Any other lessons from the ancient texts you'd care to share?"

Gabby put her hand on Sam's sleeve. "I'm sure he was just being..."

But Sam was just getting started. He removed his hand from under Gabby's, as if to say, *Don't worry, I've got this.* "Despite living a life of royalty," Sam began, in a voice loud enough for people at other tables to notice, "the Pandava brothers in the Mahabharata did not hesitate to give up all their riches and comforts to live in the wild. Of special mention is the one-year period where they lived incognito, donning various humble roles while working for a king. One of the brothers, Arjuna, lived as a music teacher, while another, Bhima, became a cook. The female protagonist Draupadi became a beautician to a princess. They all held themselves together through long periods of strife by adapting to every situation they encountered."

Joseph was intrigued. "Do you mean we should go into the field and experience what the people themselves are going through?"

Sam nodded. "Go live with the customers and the workers," he advised. "Live in their houses. See what they see. Feel what they feel."

Gabby looked at Sam and then at Joseph, the two most important men in her life at this moment. "Sam, how did you come up with this?" she asked.

"I didn't come up with anything," said Sam, humbly. "I simply took lessons from the scriptures."

Joseph looked at Sam and smiled, "I think we have our newest team member."

They clinked glasses. Joseph's budding consultancy now numbered three.

Chapter Seven

A few days later, Joseph approached a very familiar-looking house. But this wasn't just a social visit. He chose this home and neighborhood for a specific reason. He was collecting data on Pyramid.

He noticed that the paint had faded on the house, and there were a few bikes on the dusty lawn. He knocked on the door and a moment later, it opened. He was greeted by a woman with gray-streaked hair wiping her hands on her apron.

"You're early!" she exclaimed, "I thought you weren't coming for another hour!" She looked up the street. "I sure hope you didn't drive! Wouldn't want to park a fancy car around here."

"No, I got someone to drop me off," Joseph said. He saw no reason to tell her he had a car and driver at his disposal from Pyramid. "You must be Mrs. Kirkland," he added. "So nice to meet you."

She beamed. "That's me all right. Though most people call me Josie. Except for my kids, of course."

"Speaking of whom," Joseph said, noticing two small faces peering out from behind their mother.

Their mother pushed them out. "Children, introduce yourselves properly."

The boy, who seemed about nine, looked Joseph straight in the eye. "How do you do, sir? My name is John Lewis Kirkland."

"I take it you're named after—" Joseph began.

"Yes, the great civil rights leader and congressman John Lewis," the boy replied, his tone serious.

Joseph nodded. He knelt and addressed the little girl who was clinging to her mother's apron. "And who is this?"

"My name is Marion Anderson Kirkland," the little girl said softly and then gave a shy smile.

"Those are beautiful names," Joseph said.

"Do you have children, Mr. Chandler?" asked Josie Kirkland.

"Please, call me Joseph. Yes, two boys, one just about John's age. The other, a little older than Marion. My wife, Dionne, and I have our hands full, as you can imagine."

All of a sudden, Joseph felt a thudding under his feet. It brought him right back to his roots, as a car pumping out a song by rapper and singer A$AP Rocky slowly crawled by, the heavy bass line going straight through him.

Josie pursed her lips. "Those fools spend more on their cars…" she began, but before she could finish her thought, she shook her head. "Here we are, standing and talking in the doorway like you're some sort of salesman, and me not even inviting you in. Please! Please!"

She pulled at Joseph's arm, and he crossed into the living room. Josie picked up a few stray juice cans. "Please excuse the mess, Joseph. We're not used to, well, having company."

Joseph could feel his heart beating in his chest.

Josie looked around her living room. Then she looked at the man in front of her, dressed in his nice clean polo shirt and spotless chinos. "I guess you aren't used to being around folks like us either."

Joseph motioned to a well-worn chair by the television. "May I?"

"Of course!" Josie said.

Joseph settled in the seat. "Actually, Josie, if you want to know the truth, I am very used to being around 'folks like you.' My whole family is made up of folks like you. As a matter of fact, I come from right here."

The two children gazed at Joseph like he'd grown another head.

"You mean you grew up in Roseland?" John Lewis asked in a skeptical voice. "You sure don't sound like it."

Joseph drew closer. "Do you want to know a secret?"

Both children nodded solemnly.

"I grew up in this very house," Joseph said.

"Wait!" Josie exclaimed, "I heard about you! You teach up at the university, isn't that right?"

"That's correct," said Joseph.

Josie turned to her kids. "You see? This is why I keep on you to do well in school. Mr. Chandler here started off just like you two!"

"That's right!" Joseph said. "And Marion, I have two sisters. One is a lawyer and the other is a doctor. And you know why?"

Marion shook her head.

"Because we listened to our mama, that's why!" said Joseph.

He spent the rest of the afternoon going over the children's homework with them.

That night, Josie's husband, Ricky, came home. He worked as a driver for FedEx, delivering packages for several retail companies that were beating Pyramid at its own game.

As Joseph sat for dinner, he could feel Josie's discomfort at feeding him such simple fare.

"Everything is delicious," he assured her. "Best meal I've had in a long time."

Josie shook her head. "Now don't go telling fibs, Joseph. I bet you go out to fancy restaurants all the time."

Joseph thought of the upscale yet cold Signature Room, and then this beautiful family who were exactly the kind of people he'd like Pyramid to serve. "I am telling the God's honest truth, Josie. A meal isn't just what's on the plate. It's the people you share it with."

Ricky nodded. "Amen, Joseph. But be honest. No restaurant can touch her peach cobbler."

Joseph grinned. "I'm having a second helping, aren't I?" He wiped his mouth with a napkin. "You folks have been so wonderful, welcoming me into your home. I just need some honest answers."

"Well, honesty is all you're going to get from Ricky and me," Josie said, as she sat down with a glass of sweet tea next to her husband. "And we're so glad to have you."

"All right. Let's say John Lewis needed new pants for school next year. Where would you get them?"

Josie frowned. "Well, it depends. He gets most of his clothes from his cousin who's a few years older. But when we have to, we'd go to the thrift store, or maybe one of those big-box stores, if it was having a sale."

"How about things like toilet paper and kitchen supplies?" Joseph asked.

"Now, that stuff we get at the local discount market, even though the prices are higher than I'd like," Ricky admitted. "You know, for the convenience."

Joseph took a bite of his dessert. As casually as he could, he asked, "You've got a Pyramid right up the road, don't you?"

Both Rick and Josie burst out laughing.

"You couldn't pay me to shop there!" Josie said.

"I wouldn't go if they were giving stuff away for free!" added Ricky.

Then a worried expression came over his face. "You don't work for them, do you?"

"Joseph is a big professor at the university! What kind of question is that?" asked his wife.

"I'm sorry, Joseph. Sometimes Ricky worries a bit about the wrong things."

Joseph scratched his head. "Well, I *am* kind of working for Pyramid. I agreed to help the owner get good people like you to shop there again. Now if *he* were sitting here, what would you tell him?"

They sat in silence for a minute.

"You want the truth, right?" asked Ricky.

"That's what I'm here for," Joseph said. "That and the peach cobbler."

Josie looked him straight in the eye. "Okay. I would tell the 'Boss Man, 'Maybe you need to visit your stores.' Oh, forget that. He'd be treated right. But try visiting as a Black family."

"And when we need help, most of them won't even give us the time of day. It's like we're inconveniencing them," Ricky added. "They sometimes follow us around like they don't trust us."

Joseph nodded. Now he was getting somewhere. He sat back and listened as the family poured out their woes about Pyramid, a store that he loved as a child that apparently had lost not just its way but its heart. Sam was right, Joseph thought: A business is a family, whether it realizes that or not. Families are built with emotion and heart. And customers were just as much a part of the family as the workers and the stockholders. This was going to be a very educational evening.

"Tell me more," Joseph said, and Ricky and Josie did just that.

Chapter Eight

Darpan Bhalla wearily opened his front door. He sighed as he took off his shirt with the patch "Pyramid Security" sewn on the sleeve. The less time he needed to wear that shirt, the better it suited him. He hung up his hat and belt and put on his favorite sweater, the one he had bought on his last trip back home to Manali, in northern India.

He stiffened as he heard a strange voice in the living room.

A man's voice. In his house?

He checked his watch. He wasn't early.

Chhaya had never given him reason to suspect her fidelity. But she was still a beauty. With a wife like his, a man must always be on his guard.

But Darpan had so many questions! Allowing a strange man into his home without asking? This had never happened before. He was about to call out when his wife quietly came around the corner and spotted him.

Before he could ask her, she held her finger up to her lips as if to say, *Hush dear, all will be explained in time.*

"Chhaya, I must insist you—"

"Shh!" she said. She took his hand and kissed it. "Come listen!" she whispered.

In the other room, two children were being held spellbound by a young man who was in the middle of telling them a story.

"Lord Dronacharya gathered all his subjects and asked them to strike the eye of the wooden bird. But before they could shoot their arrows, he asked each one of them a question. He first called and asked Yudhisthir, the eldest, 'What do you see there?' Yudhisthir answered, 'I see a wooden bird, the branch and the tree, the leaves moving, and other birds.'"

Darpan smiled. This was one of his favorite stories from the Mahabharata—*Arjun and the Bird's Eye Test*. The young man was a wonderful storyteller, bringing the tale to life with different voices for the great Lord, and for Arjun and the others.

"Everyone else who followed said just the same thing, 'I see a wooden bird, the branch and the tree, the leaves moving and other birds.' And after each reply, Dronacharya asked each one to lay down his bow and arrow. Then it was Arjun's turn. Do you know what he said?"

The two children shook their heads.

The young man smiled. "Arjun did *not* say what the others said. He replied to his Lord, 'I can only see the eye of the bird.' The great Lord Dronacharya smiled, for it showed him that he was right in favoring Arjun. All the others had set their eyes on everything, but Arjuna had only set his eyes on his goal—the eye of the bird," he said.

The children clapped. The young man bowed as Darpan and Chhaya came into the room. "I am so sorry, sir. I did not know you had arrived," he said.

Darpan extended his hand. "You are welcome, of course. I'm Darpan Bhalla."

"Samesh Bhati," said the young man, and took the older man's hand in his. "An honor to meet you."

Darpan laughed. "I am sure you have not come into our home just to tell our children tales from the Mahabharata."

Chhaya broke in. "Samesh has come to talk to us about our jobs."

A worried look came over Darpan's face. "There is something wrong? Are we going to be let go?"

Sam stopped him. "No, nothing like that, I promise you. I, well, the CEO of Pyramid has hired me to come and talk to you and your wife, since you both work there."

From the kitchen, the warm, fragrant smell of Channa Madra curry and yogurt filled the air.

"We eat first, and then we talk," Darpan said.

Sam nodded. "I haven't had a home-cooked meal since I was back in Bengaluru."

Darpan's face broke out in a smile. "Bengaluru? We are from Manali!"

"Practically neighbors!" exclaimed Chhaya as she doled out the Tudkiya Bhath.

The children giggled as they watched Sam dig into the delicious food set in front of him.

Their father shook his head. "I see you've met Raj and Anitha."

"He tells great stories, Baba!" said Anitha.

After they ate, Sam turned to the children. "And now it is time for your parents to tell *me* some stories."

As soon as the dishes were cleared, and the tea was served, the grownups gathered in the living room of the simple house.

Darpan cleared his throat. "Is there something we will have to sign?"

"Not at all. This is all confidential. Just for my own research," Sam assured him.

He turned to Chhaya. "Now you work as a cashier. Can you describe your store?"

Chhaya reddened. "It is hard for me to say..."

"Please," Sam insisted gently. "It is important for us to provide the CEO with what he needs to know. I think he is like the archers in my story. He sees all the details but has taken his eye off the ultimate goal. It is my hope that in talking to people like you that we can help him be more like Arjun and concentrate on what has to be done."

"All right," said Chhaya. "If you must know, the store is dirty and unpleasant. I wouldn't shop there or set foot in it if I wasn't being paid."

"And being paid poorly, as well!" Darpan added.

Sam turned to him. "And you? How is it, being a security guard?"

Darpan sighed. "All day long homeless people wander into the store and sometimes sleep in the back areas. The manager doesn't seem to care. We do what we can, but honestly, people just don't feel secure in our store."

Sam looked carefully at Darpan and Chhaya, at their spotless home, their well-behaved children. He saw two people who were hard-working and proud. They deserved better. And Sam was determined to help them get it.

Chapter Nine

"In one hundred feet, turn left! You have reached your destination!" sang out the chirpy voice of Google Maps as Gabby turned the wheel and entered the driveway of 1022 Laurel Avenue. A modest house for Evanston, it was a simple ranch with a two-car garage. Gabby pulled in and stopped the car. Since her hometown of Winnetka was only a few miles away, and she had friends who lived in Evanston, this was familiar territory for her.

She got out of the car and stretched. She was a little early for her appointment with Richard Fassler, who supplied picture frames for most of the Pyramid stores in Illinois, and much of the upper Midwest. He was the perfect representative of the smaller businessman who Pyramid dealt with on a daily basis and who'd become disenchanted with their attitude.

A familiar sound met Gabby's ears. Her heart started to race as she heard the familiar *thwump thwump thwump* noise of a ball that had become the music of the suburban tree-lined streets for decades. She rounded the house to see the regulation-size basketball hoop erected by the garage, as it had been at the house where she grew up.

A young woman whom Gabby guessed to be about seventeen was shooting baskets. She was sweating, and Gabby noticed a Northwestern sweatshirt discarded in a heap on the grass nearby.

The young woman stopped and stared at Gabby. "Can I help you?" she asked.

"I'm here to see Mr. Fassler," Gabby replied.

The girl picked up a towel and wiped her face. "That's my dad. He's not here yet."

Gabby smiled. "So, I gathered. Do you mind if I wait here?"

"Suit yourself," the girl said.

Gabby picked up the basketball and bounced it a few times. "You're pretty good, you know."

"Thanks. I made varsity this year. Just working on my skills," the girl said, proudly.

Gabby threw her the ball. "But I noticed when you shoot, the ball sits on the tip of your thumb."

The girl looked annoyed. "So?"

Gabby motioned for the girl to throw the ball back, which she did, *hard*. Gabby caught it easily and held it in her hand. "You need to have the ball rest on the side of the thumb rather than on the tip of the thumb on every shot. It may feel awkward at first, but it will really help, and more of your shots will hit the dead center of the rim."

She tossed the ball effortlessly and watched with satisfaction as it sailed into the net.

The girl eyed her. "What are you, like a coach or something?"

"No, just someone who loves to play, like you," Gabby said, laughing. "What's your name, by the way?"

"Kendra," said the girl as she dribbled the ball. "You?"

"Gabrielle Richardson, but everyone calls me Gabby," Gabby answered. She tapped the ball away from Kendra and went in for an easy layup. Then she tossed the ball back. "Your turn."

Kendra looked her in the eye with an expression of determination Gabby knew well. *This girl will be a champion,* she thought as Kendra pushed past her to make the basket.

"You played in college, or just high school?" Kendra asked.

At this point, it was clear they were about to have a one-on-one. Gabby was glad she hadn't changed into her high heels when she came out of the car. She had an easy three inches on the girl, but she had to admit, Kendra had moves. By the time Dick Fassler's Acura pulled into the driveway, the two had been playing for fifteen minutes. Gabby was up by two points.

Dick, an ex-jock, now had the body of someone who'd had a few too many deep-dish pizzas and beers. He stared in wonder at the two women battling it out in front of him.

"Mr. Fassler?" Gabby panted, looking over at him.

"I take it you're Gabby Richardson," he said.

Gabby threw up a three-pointer and turned to greet him. "That's me."

"You, uh, want to finish that? I can wait," Dick said. "What's the score?"

His daughter grabbed the ball. "25-20."

"Who's winning?" he asked.

Kendra pointed to Gabby. "She is."

A grin spread across her father's face. "You giving her a spanking?"

Gabby shook her head. "Nope. She's good, really good."

"Better be careful, Kendra hates to lose," Dick said.

"Sounds familiar," Gabby said. She turned to Kendra. "We can finish this another time. I promise."

Kendra dropped the ball on the ground. "Whatever."

Gabby could tell she hated to lose.

Dick opened the front door. He motioned Gabby in. "Shall we?"

Gabby nodded and followed him. As they got to the entrance, Kendra pushed past her.

"Young lady, not even an 'excuse me'?" asked her father.

"If you'd have come home fifteen minutes later, I would have won," she muttered.

Gabby tried not to smile. She knew exactly how the girl felt.

"I don't think so, young lady," Dick said. "Do you realize you've been playing against someone who won a silver medal in the Olympics?"

Gabby felt her jaw clench. He had to bring that up. She was sure Kendra was going to make a snide remark about how Gabby was such a loser since she didn't get the gold.

To her surprise, Kendra just stopped and stared. "What? Are you kidding me? That is so cool!"

Gabby looked at the girl. Kendra's eyes were glowing. "I can't believe I played basketball against an Olympian!"

"It wasn't basketball," Gabby began. "It was the heptathlon—"

"Wow, that's like the hardest sport of all!" Kendra practically shouted. "I know all about it!" She grabbed her phone for a picture. "Do you mind?"

"Of course not," Gabby said as she posed for a selfie with her young fan.

"Do I get major dad points for bringing her here?" Dick asked as he brought in some soda cans from the kitchen.

Kendra held her cool glass up to her forehead. "You would have gotten more dad points if you weren't late. Anyway, I have some calc homework I need to get to. And I think Dad wants to have his meeting. It was so great meeting you, though!"

With that Kendra bounded up the stairs, with the same loping gait Gabby knew so well.

"You too!" she called after her.

. . .

Gabby sat with Dick for a few hours, hearing all his complaints about working with Pyramid.

"You know how much I depend on Pyramid's business, but a lot of us feel we're being asked to shoulder the burden of bad decisions that management has made," Dick told her.

"I hear you," Gabby said.

"Yeah, but do they?" he asked. "You're probably the sixth consultant I've talked to. They make big promises, but nothing changes."

And that, Gabby thought to herself, *was the problem.* "Could you give me some specifics?" she asked, taking out her laptop.

"I could give you specifics for the next hour," he said. "Or two hours. Or three."

"I've got nothing but time," Gabby replied, sitting down. "Let's get into it."

Chapter Ten

Thelma Halverson smiled at the three people sitting patiently in her waiting area. "As soon as he's off the phone, I'll be sure and let him know you're here." She stared at them and thought to herself, *Waiting all this time. Just like all the others, thinking they can help Mr. Collinsworth with his problems.*

Thelma liked Mr. Collinsworth. Unlike all those McCormacks, he remembered her name. Imagine that! You've got an executive assistant and you don't even bother to learn her name. And in the fifteen years that Thelma had been working at Pyramid HQ, Skip was the first CEO to give her a present on her birthday! Thelma looked at the coffee mug on her desk and sighed. It had the Chicago Bears logo on its side. He knew she was a diehard fan. It even came with a little teddy bear in a football jersey!

Too bad he would be gone soon, she said to herself. Then she'll probably be stuck with another McCormack as CEO, no doubt.

Thelma looked at the Black gentleman and felt sad for him and the tall girl he'd brought with him before, driving down to the office. This time they brought someone new—a skinny young Indian man, who looked very serious. He was filling out some sort of puzzle, and occasionally the blonde girl would lean over and point at one of the answers and he would nod.

When Skip's phone light went out, Thelma immediately picked up and let him know his three o'clock was here. "He says to go on in," she informed them, putting down the phone.

They trouped into his office.

Thelma shook her head again. *Seem like such nice folks. A real shame there's nothing they can do.*

Skip rose from his desk to greet Joseph, Gabby, and Sam. "I'm so sorry. That was one of the stockholders. One of the *big* stockholders. It seems like the main part of my job these days is to keep them from jumping out of windows."

Joseph laughed and shook his hand. "I've always said half of being a good CEO is being a cheerleader."

"What's the other half?" asked Skip.

Joseph smiled and took a seat across the desk. "That's what we're here to talk to you about."

"Don't get freaked out by the carpet," Gabby whispered to Sam. "I know it's kind of loud."

"No, it's fine," murmured Sam. "It reminds me of my Auntie Pooja's house. I think even the garage was this color."

Skip came over and greeted Sam. "Welcome," he said. I don't believe we've met. I'm Skip Collinsworth."

"Delighted to meet you," Sam said. "I'm Samesh Bhati."

Skip sat at his desk, then turned toward Sam. "So, are you in business school with Gabrielle here?"

"No, he's my boyfriend," Gabby explained. "He's a doctoral candidate in Ancient Indian Literature at the university."

Skip turned and looked at Joseph with an expression that clearly read, *What is this guy doing here exactly?*

Joseph held up his hand. "All will be explained in time, I promise."

Skip leaned back in his chair. "I can't wait."

"I call dibs on the recliner!" Gabby shouted and jumped on her old friend, the La-Z-Boy.

Sam snorted. "I didn't want to sit there anyway," he said and sat stiffly next to Joseph.

Sam leaned in toward Skip. "She makes everything a game. And she hates to lose."

"So I've noticed," Skip said, laughing.

Joseph put his briefcase on his lap and briskly snapped it open. He removed a slim file and put it on the top of the desk.

Skip regarded the file with interest. "So, this is the answer? This is the magic bullet that's going to save Pyramid?"

Joseph nodded. "If this doesn't do it, nothing will." He slid the folder across the desktop.

Skip picked it up and opened it. He was surprised to find just one sheet of paper. He looked up, confused. "So, where's the PowerPoint presentation, with the deck—the one that explains this?"

Joseph shook his head. "No presentation. No charts. No deck. This is it. The whole thing."

Skip's expression changed. "Is this some sort of joke?" he demanded. He looked over at Joseph, who wasn't smiling.

"I've never been more serious about anything in my life," Joseph said.

Skip slammed the folder onto his desk. "There's one word written here!"

"And what is that one word?" asked Sam, in a soft voice.

Skip looked again. "Well, it's ... trust." His face darkened. "Really? Really? Two weeks of work and this is what you give me? Boy, I really got my money's worth."

Joseph's voice was steady as he answered. "If I may remind

you, I haven't asked for a penny from you. And I won't unless I can help you turn this company around."

Skip stared at Joseph for a moment. Finally, he chuckled. "That's one hell of a business model." He looked down at the paper, with its one word staring back at him, mocking him. "Well, I guess you get what you pay for, huh?"

Gabby stared at Joseph and marveled at his ability to exude calm and confidence at a moment like this. She would have walked out of the room by now if it were up to her. *Screw this guy if he doesn't want our help*, she thought.

Joseph looked Skip straight in the eye. It was a little intimidating to face someone so sure of himself. "Trust isn't just a word on a page, Skip. It's the secret to getting Pyramid back on its feet. But it has to start now. You have to trust *me*, trust that I wouldn't have come if I didn't think I could help you. And I brought Gabby and Sam because I trust their perspectives. The diversity of our combined thinking plus the insights we've gleaned from ethnographies with Pyramid stakeholders has been critical in forming this answer."

Skip looked down at the paper. "Okay, let me take a step back and regain my composure." He took a brief moment, and then said, "So ... trust. Trust isn't just given, it's earned, right?"

Joseph nodded.

Skip leaned back in his chair again. "You can start by earning *my* trust. And to be frank, you're doing a lousy job so far."

"Our journey to choosing this word to share with you," Joseph began, "started when we went and spent time with some of your customers, employees, and suppliers. This ethnographic approach was inspired by Sam and fit right in with Gabby's passion for unearthing human-centered insights."

Gabby nodded. "One of the very first axioms we learn in sociology is, 'Start where people are.' You can't figure out how to help them by sitting in an office and looking at spreadsheets."

Joseph looked at the young man next to him. "Sam here spends most of his day studying a manuscript from over a thousand years ago, which still guides the spiritual life of billions of people."

Skip had a cut-to-the-chase look on his face. "Yeah, I know. I must have read a dozen or so books about business lessons derived from different historical narratives over the years. I get it. So, how does that help me now?"

"What I study every day cannot be boiled down into simple slogans and easy truisms," Sam told him. "There is a deep spiritual component to what is wrong with your company if you don't mind my saying so, sir."

Skip opened his mouth to answer and then changed his mind. He gestured for Sam to go on.

Sam stood up. He placed his hands behind his back, like the honor student he was. "The people I met said they feel empty. They aren't appreciated by their employer; they are made to feel like cogs in a machine, replaceable, and irrelevant."

Skip nodded. "With all due respect, Mr. Bhati, they aren't the only ones who are replaceable. *I* need to show results."

"But it starts with your employees trusting that the company truly *cares* for them," insisted Sam. "The most critical thing you need to address is the fact that for your customers to come to Pyramid, you need your suppliers to respect you, and your employees to love you."

Joseph nodded, and Sam sat down.

"Societies run on trust," Gabby added. "All successful organizations ultimately learn this lesson. This is the foundation of the entire field of sociology. Fear and intimidation only take you so far with employees and suppliers."

Skip laughed. "I can name you a dozen *Fortune* 500 companies that would disagree with you."

"Sure, that may work for a while," Joseph agreed. "But once the company begins to lose market share, or there is a change in management, those companies struggle. We have a plan."

"I'm all ears," Skip said, but he still sounded skeptical.

"I don't want to disparage the work that has been done so far," Joseph began. "But everything we've seen indicates a focus on tactical thinking. Nobody's looking at the big picture. And at the center of that big picture is an overwhelming lack of *trust*." Joseph paused to let his words sink in, and then he continued. "Without a foundation of trust, all the efforts in the world regarding price sensitivity or operational improvements, or what products and brands to offer will be meaningless. All that amounts to is rearranging deck chairs on the Titanic."

"This captain isn't going down with the ship," Skip said, laughing. "Because this ship isn't going down!"

"The definition of trust is based on a very simple formula—set clear expectations and consistently meet/exceed those expectations—that is the foundation of trust."

"And it's not the big things you do that matter. Everyone does the big things reasonably well. It's the little things that create and restore trust," Gabby added. "Things like, get the bathrooms clean, get the lighting right, make sure the stores are safe, employ people who smile. All of those seemingly small things amount to a lot for many people. Trust isn't a slogan. You earn it by the actions you take that show you care about the people who shop in your stores *and* the people who work there."

"And it needs to start from the top. You have to set clear expectations and you have to lead from the front. This involves you getting in there and convincing your employees, your customers, and your suppliers to trust you," Joseph told him.

Skip snorted. "Well, if that's all I have to do…"

"We're telling you that trust has to be more than just a slogan or a word on a PR document," Gabby said. "It has to go deeper than that. It has to be something *you* are invested in."

"You know about Paul O'Neill, the former head of Alcoa, right?" Joseph asked Skip.

"Yeah, I remember he made a big deal about safety and accident rates, right?" Skip replied.

"It wasn't just a 'big deal,'" Joseph told him. "From his first speech as CEO, he made it his number one priority. His goal was to make Alcoa the benchmark for worker safety. He stated that there was no such thing as 'acceptable risk.' And he meant it. Do you know what he told his management team when one of his workers died in an accident?"

"He didn't say 'Well, accidents happen,'" Gabby said.

"He didn't just pay off the poor man's widow and family to make it go away," Sam added.

Joseph quickly took another piece of paper out of his briefcase. He wanted to get this right, word for word. "He told them: 'We killed this man. It's my failure of leadership. I caused his death. And it's the failure of all of you in the chain of command.'"

Skip nodded. "So, you're saying trust has to start at the top."

Joseph put the paper back in his briefcase and paused.

Sam turned to Skip. "Think of what it would mean to the people you work with, for them to be able to be proud to work at Pyramid again, for them to know that they have a leader they can trust. No battle is won by armies which do not trust and respect their Lord enough to die for them."

Skip pondered this for a moment. "I appreciate the history lessons, folks," he said thoughtfully. "And the sociology lecture.

But even if you're right, that stuff is still theoretical 'warm fuzzies.' I need practical solutions."

"In case you've forgotten," Joseph interjected. "I've spent my time in the trenches just like you. I'm not here to blow smoke, Skip. We have a road map, a series of practical jobs to be done. But to get us there, we need a lodestar to guide us. Trust is that guiding light, the principle that is the foundation for every action moving forward. Either you understand that, or..." Joseph checked his watch and breathed out dramatically. "We leave now and beat the traffic."

Skip looked at Gabby. "You feel the same way, huh?"

She nodded.

His gaze turned to Sam.

"I sense you have doubts," Sam said.

Skip smiled and looked at the single piece of paper on his desk that looked more naked than ever. "That's putting it mildly."

"Neither in this world nor elsewhere is there any happiness in store for the man who always doubts," Sam said, solemnly.

"Let me guess, the Mahabharata?" Skip asked.

Sam smiled. "Of course, from the Bhagavad Gita."

Skip took a moment. He thought of his wife. He thought of his customers, his employees, and all that they had been through. The challenges the company had inflicted on suppliers, punishing them for every bad decision made by an executive, the lack of taking responsibility by every person who had sat in that same chair before him and stared at the carpet. It would end with him. "Okay, I'm in," Skip finally said, calmly.

Joseph's face broke out in a smile—a real smile, the first since he'd gotten to the office. "And now we get to work," he said.

Skip shook his hand. "This is going to cost a lot of money to fix, isn't it?"

"I can't see any other way," Joseph admitted.

"So, let's get to it!" Gabby declared, enthusiastically.

"Not so fast," Skip said. "You've forgotten one thing. I can only do so much as CEO. I've got to get the Board behind me."

Gabby made a face. "Uh-oh."

Sam looked confused. "But once you explain it to them, they will certainly see it is to their benefit, as you have done?"

"The only thing that is to their benefit is making money," Skip said, grimly. "I'm going to have to convince them somehow that spending the money will be worth it. This isn't going to be easy."

Joseph looked him in the eye. His gaze was unflinching. "You have a clear pathway and a team with you now. We'll do everything we can to help you prepare for whatever they throw at you."

"You don't know the McCormack family," Skip said.

Joseph sat down. He pulled out his iPad from his briefcase. "Not yet. But you're going to tell us everything you know. And by the time we leave, we will."

Chapter Eleven

Nothing could have been further from the Pyramid offices than the glitzy Florentine Room at the Intercontinental. Located in the heart of San Francisco, it was a testament to the life that some of the McCormacks chose to lead. Gold moiré drapery, crystal chandeliers, and high windows that would put Versailles to shame.

By the time Skip and his wife, Jenna McCormack, arrived for the quarterly meeting of the Board, many of their colleagues had already ensconced themselves around the great room. There were flurries of conversation punctuated with howls of laughter. Every once in a while, certain statements would linger in the air, such as "Aspen this year was a *hoot*!" or "We missed you in Nice, darling!"

Joseph's appearance alongside Skip did not go unnoticed. There were some raised eyebrows, but everyone was too polite to make a scene about it. There would be plenty of time for that during the official meeting.

Jenna kissed Skip on the cheek. "Time for me to earn my combat pay. I need to mingle and shore up the troops."

"Go get 'em, girl," Skip said, giving her arm a squeeze. He knew she'd been working the phone all week trying to get the younger McCormacks on board with Skip's plans. They would need every vote they could get to make it happen. Jenna had her mother's proxy vote, and Skip knew that a number of her cousins were also representing their respective branches of the family.

"How does it look?" Joseph asked.

Skip noticed a large, imposing presence in the corner, in deep consultation with a small, ferret-faced man. He winced. "Damn. That's Rockwell and Rand Swigert. I didn't think they'd be here."

"Rand Swigert?" asked Joseph. "The CFO?"

Skip nodded. "He had gallbladder surgery just two weeks ago. His presence here complicates things."

Joseph didn't need to have it spelled out for him. Rand had been angling for the CEO's office for the last three years, insinuating himself into the good graces of the most powerful and involved of the McCormack clan. It was no secret that he was furious that the family had chosen Skip as the first outsider to run the firm. He was Rockwell's closest advisor, and the most brutal when it came to cost-cutting measures.

"Look sharp, here they come," muttered Skip, as Rockwell maneuvered his bulk through the room, with his smaller *consigliere* in tow.

"Skip!" boomed Rockwell, extending a large, bearlike hand. "So nice of you to grace us with your presence! I didn't think anything could pry you out of the loving arms of the Fuller Park HQ."

He leaned in as if he was giving Skip a brilliant gem of insight for his ears only. "You know, when I was CEO, they couldn't get me to go out there at gunpoint. I guess you have a stronger stomach for those rundown office spaces than some of us. Still, good to see you!"

"Wouldn't miss it for the world," Skip replied, doing his best to return the crushing grip of Rockwell McCormack. "And you're looking well, Rand."

Joseph decided that Rand had what could only be described as a resting sneer face.

"Wonderful what modern medicine can do these days, isn't it?" Rand said. "Just last week I was stuck in a hospital bed with tubes stuck up my—"

"Yes, well," Rockwell interjected. "We don't have to go into that. Let's just say Rand knows when he is needed."

"Right," Rand said. "Here I am! Good to go!"

Rockwell peered at Joseph. "And who have *you* brought along? I don't believe we've met."

Skip turned to Joseph. "This is Joseph Chandler. I've brought him on as a consultant."

Rockwell sighed. "Oh, dear. Another one. Pardon me, Mr. Chambers, is it?"

"Chandler," Joseph said with a fake smile.

"You'll forgive me if I don't remember your name," Rockwell went on. "But there have been *so many* consultants parading around this company. They come and go so fast—*so many.*"

"And with so little good advice," added Rand.

The two men laughed and Rockwell downed what was left of his drink. He made a small bow. "Well, gents, I think there's just time enough before the meeting to order a refill. What're you drinking, Skip?"

"I'm keeping to water, thanks," Skip replied.

"I guess you're saving your drinking until after the meeting," Rand smirked. "When you'll need it."

"I suppose you're not a drinking man either, Mr. Chapman?" Rockwell asked.

Joseph shook his head, a tight smile planted firmly on his

lips. He was about to correct Rockwell again but knew that this was all part of the game.

Rockwell turned and shrugged. "Off we go in search of more liquid sustenance. Will you excuse us, gentlemen?"

With that, he and Rand swept past the less significant McCormacks, resembling a large ocean liner with its tiny dinghy in tow in its wake.

Skip turned to Joseph. "Don't be fooled. Rockwell talks big, but it's Rand who pulls the strings. He's the one we have to look out for."

Jenna returned, looking flushed. "I think we're okay. The cousins I've spoken to are willing to listen to what you have to say."

"That's all I can ask for right now," said Skip. "We just want a chance to tell them why they should trust us and our plan. Then, it's up to them."

A tinkling sound emanated from the large oval table, as Letitia, "Letty" McCormack, the elderly daughter of Trader Larry and current Chairperson, tapped her fork against her glass. "Ladies and gentlemen," she called out. "I believe it's time we bring this meeting to order."

As the various family members and their counselors took their seats, Skip grabbed Jenna's hand. "Well, darling. *Ave, Imperator, morituri te salutant.*"

Joseph hadn't studied Latin in years, but even he knew what that meant: *Hail, Emperor, those who are about to die salute you!*

Chapter Twelve

As the meeting progressed, Joseph did all he could to not have his facial expression resemble a grimace. First off was the treasurer's report, which could only have been gloomier if an actual storm cloud appeared over the room.

Then there was an overall review of how the company's stores were performing by geographic area. Nearly every store was underwater. It seemed that this was news to no one, and no one seemed terribly concerned.

Finally, Letitia turned to Skip. "And now, we have what I believe is called—*ahem*—'A strategic plan of action to positively affect the growth of Pyramid's main assets,' from our new CEO, Skip Collinsworth!"

There was a general clinking as the assembled McCormacks tapped their glasses of Mouton-Rothschild 2016 ($1,000 a bottle, and not available at Pyramid stores).

Skip stood up. "Thank you, Aunt Letty. I think after those reports, it is no secret that, as of now, Pyramid is underperforming in practically every way."

"And whose fault is that?" asked a voice from the other end of the table. Skip didn't have to look to see that it was Rockwell.

"I think there's no need to point fingers," Skip continued. "There's enough blame to go around for everyone who's sat in the CEO seat since Trader Larry departed. I'm assuming I don't need to give examples?"

There was an uncomfortable shifting in the chairs around the table. Many of the people there had already had their turn running the company and only ended up worsening the problem.

Skip looked around the room. "What I am about to propose to you is going to seem audacious, but I think we can all agree that something drastic has to be done to save this company."

"Excuse me, but we *don't* all agree," said a bespectacled McCormack with a tasteful silver haircut. This was Gregor McCormack, Letitia's son. "I mean, let's discuss this. Market forces are what control the stock prices, correct? We need to simply show the market that we're doing *something*."

"Look, a Band-Aid isn't going to be enough in this situation," Skip protested.

"Who said anything about a Band-Aid?" Gregor said, his voice rising. "Let's just be clear about what the problem is —*unions*. They're bleeding us dry."

Joseph raised his hand. "With all due respect, less than one-fourth of all Pyramid employees are unionized. As a matter of fact, you've spent more money on hiring anti-union consultants than on any improvements to your stores."

"For those who haven't met him yet, this is Joseph Chandler. He is a professor from the Booth School of Business, and he has helped us develop the plan to get this company back on its feet."

Deathly silence. Joseph could feel dozens of unfriendly pairs of eyes boring into him. He nodded and smiled.

"So, what's your plan, or is it a big secret?" asked Rand.

"Before I give you the details," Skip replied, "I need to talk about changing our thinking and taking our corporate philosophy to a new place."

"Excellent!" exclaimed Rockwell. "I couldn't agree more!"

Before Skip could interrupt, Rand had taken out stacks of paper and began handing them out to all the participants in the room.

"Rand and I put our heads together and came up with the perfect solution to Pyramid's problems. One that will raise $1 billion in capital and make our company the darling of Wall Street once again," Rockwell announced, grandly.

Joseph glanced at the paper he had been handed. He ran a hand over his mouth, trying to hide the shock. Rand was trying to cut Skip off at the knees with his own proposal.

Skip stared at Rockwell in disbelief. "You can't be serious."

Rand addressed the gathered McCormacks. "I'll just summarize what's here, so we don't have to waste time with the details. What you're seeing is the current market value for all the properties that Pyramid owns and those that we rent out to our franchises."

Letitia nodded. "That's quite a lot of money."

"It certainly is," Rand continued. "We propose selling off all our physical stores and operating as a completely digital entity."

There were suddenly voices speaking all at once in the room.

Letitia stood up, turned to Rockwell, and the commotion died down. Her voice was ice cold. "I think I speak for all of us when I say I am disappointed in you, Rockwell. Pyramid has always prided itself on being part of the community. How dare you suggest we simply abandon our customers."

Rockwell took her criticism stoically. He knew there would be opposition.

"Well, how about this?" asked a middle-aged woman who

Skip knew was Letitia's cousin Roberta. "It seems to me that we need to find people who *want* to work. I was speaking with one of the cleaning ladies on my staff and she said when she went to get supplies at the store, the associates barely acknowledged her."

"So, you're saying fire all the employees?" asked Skip.

"I mean, why not? Then they can get welfare. That's what they want, isn't it?" asked Roberta. She looked at Joseph. "No offense."

Years of self-control had trained Joseph not to rise to the bait. "If I may, Mrs. McCormack," Joseph began.

"Mrs. Kaiser," she corrected him.

"My apologies, Mrs. Kaiser," Joseph said. "You speak of your employees like they are nothing but interchangeable blocks. These are *people*, hardworking people. Some of them have given their whole lives to Pyramid. If they feel like the company doesn't care for them, why should they care for the company?"

Roberta shrugged.

"May I ask you a question?" Joseph said.

Roberta nodded. "By all means."

Joseph gave her a polite smile. "Are you happy with your staff?"

"My staff is excellent," Roberta said. "And very happy, *and* hardworking."

Joseph stroked his chin. "You mentioned that one of your housekeepers complained about the store."

"That's right," Roberta said.

"And do you happen to know her name?"

Roberta's eyes narrowed. "I know what you're trying to do. Well, it won't work. I know her name. It's Juanita. You see, I *do* care about people when they do a good job."

There was a tug on her sleeve. Her daughter, a small, shy girl right out of college spoke up. "Actually, Mother, her name is Rosa," she said meekly.

Roberta turned a color of red not unlike the fine wine in her glass.

One of the youngest McCormacks, Shania, stood up. Joseph observed that she looked to be in her mid-to-late twenties and had a piercing in her nose.

"Great Aunt Letty," she began. "You said you spoke for all of us. Well, you do *not* speak for all of us. I want to return to Cousin Rockwell's offer. Aunt Letty, you talked about abandoning our customers. The truth is our customers abandoned us long ago. They're shopping at the online stores of our competitors. That sadly is the reality today. We can sit here and continue as we are—like buggy-whip salesmen at a car show—or we can face the facts as they are, address the future as it will be, not as we wish it to be."

Jenna stood up. "People like the ease of shopping online, but they also want the convenience of a store where they live, and the feeling of community, just like Aunt Letty said."

Aunt Letty beamed at her.

Skip squeezed Jenna's shoulder. What would he do without her? "Look, here's the thing," Skip said to Shania. "We do need a vibrant digital presence. That's clear."

Shania nodded.

"We have an online store already," Rand said.

Joseph handed Skip a sheet of paper, who glanced at it and then turned to Shania. "Have you visited the site?" asked Skip.

Shania looked uncomfortable. "Um, no, I was planning to."

"Don't bother," Skip said. "I don't know who hired these people, but the current Pyramid website is one of the most ineffective sites in the industry. Cumbersome menus, a clumsy search engine, and the checkout process is interminable. Not to mention it has the lowest uptime performance of any retail e-commerce site."

Rockwell downed another glass of wine, then patted his lips with a napkin. "So, young genius, what is *your* master plan? You're awfully good at poking holes in other people's ideas. What's yours?"

Skip took a moment. He felt the weight of the moment. *I need to put this just right,* he said to himself. "Our company has three constituencies—our guests, our employees, and our supplier partners. We haven't done right by any of them in a long time."

The room was silent.

Skip put his hands on the table and leaned forward. "Here's what needs to happen. We need to restore trust with all of them. If people don't trust our company, we don't stand a chance of being around. It's as simple as that. Successful businesses build strong relationships with the people who work for them, the people who supply them, and the people who buy from them. Those relationships are strengthened only when we create and maintain that trust. So, employees have to know that we respect them and we need to treat them like the valued assets they are. Any manager who doesn't see this needs to be fired. And suppliers need to trust that we're in this together and that we're not going to penalize them for our bad business decisions."

There was some nodding of heads around the table.

"And finally," Skip went on, his voice rising. "We need to take responsibility for our problems and failures and then resolve them quickly with action, so they know we care. We want our guests to feel confident that when they come to Pyramid, they're going to find a clean, well-laid-out, friction-free shopping environment, whether it's in our brick-and-mortar locations or on our site.

We want them to feel like they're treated as a person, as if they are the most valued guest, from the first moment of contact to the last. We should provide them with the best customer service that wows them every time. That's how we build trust with the people who buy our products. When they trust us and know they can rely on us, they will joyfully come back again and again. They will spread the word to others as our brand ambassadors. Our reputation then improves by leaps and bounds, our sales climb in each store and online, and we're taken seriously again in the marketplace and on Wall Street. Our vision is to go from the uninspiring experience we deliver today to an unbelievable, second-to-none that we will deliver tomorrow. That's what I want to try and do."

There was applause around the table.

Jenna was glowing.

Skip could feel himself breathing again.

He looked down at Joseph who was mouthing the words "Nice job, man."

And then Rockwell's voice boomed out from the other end of the table. "Nice words. Very inspiring. But how exactly do you plan on regaining this 'trust' you think is so important?"

"I'm not going to lie to you," Skip told the assembled McCormacks. "This is going to be a ton of hard work and will require significant resources. We need to invest in our stores. We need to invest in our people. We need to rebuild relationships with our suppliers. We need to show that these are more than empty words or proclamations. This is not about a slick marketing campaign. It's about rolling up our sleeves, getting into the trenches, and working hard with the people on the ground to win back their trust."

Rockwell laughed. "*Our* sleeves? And who, pray tell, is *us*?"

Skip put his hand on Joseph's shoulder. "This transformation has to start from the inside out. It has to start from the top. We need to get our people aligned and excited. We need to inspire them to do the right thing. We need to get in the trenches with them. That is my approach." Skip stopped to take a breath.

Rockwell jumped right back in. *"Trenches? You're going that low?"*

"I plan to lead from the front. We, as a family of owners, need to demonstrate to our people that we understand, empathize, and relate with them and their communities. That we trust our senior managers, middle managers, and employees at all levels. We need to empower them and give them the resources to do the best they can." Skip paused to get input.

Joseph used this moment to establish a contextual foundation. "The best-performing companies, ones that deliver consistently powerful results, follow this principle. If you do this, your people will not only want to improve their performance but will help you make improvements everywhere. It will build a culture of trust throughout the company and become a self-sustaining engine to drive growth. This is how Trader Larry built this icon."

Skip closed this avenue of discussion down. "A company is only as strong as the people who work for it. Let's start and show them we care about them and we trust them so they can be the foundation to support the weight of our expectations."

Heads nodded again around the room and people quickly whispered amongst themselves.

"I already have a team of our associates who are passionate about the business and are working on what we need to do to bring back our glory days," said Skip. "They are designing programs to activate insights that will transform the Pyramid model to deliver sustained profitable growth in this continually reshaping world."

"How much, Skip?" asked Letitia, cutting to the chase.

"Well, big problems need big pockets," replied Skip. "We're asking for $100 million."

There was a collective gasp.

Rand raised his hand. "Impossible!" he shouted. "That's just throwing good money after bad! I need to speak up here. What this young man is suggesting is nothing more than a vanity project, something for him to do instead of the hard work of cutting costs and closing stores. That's how you show Wall Street you mean business, not this new-age garbage. Trust? Wall Street doesn't trust anyone! And they certainly won't trust this crazy idea!"

There were murmurs of assent from the older McCormacks in the room.

"All right," Skip said evenly. "You've said your piece and I've said mine. I'll go even further. If I can't raise the earnings of Pyramid by the next shareholder's meeting six months from now, I'll quit and appoint you, Rand Swigert, as CEO. How does that sound?"

Rand looked stunned. He turned to Rockwell, who seemed bored by the whole thing. Then he turned back to Skip. "I don't see any reason why I should go along with this. You'll fail either way. And if we *don't* do as you say, we're not out $100 million."

"Fine," Skip said. "We'll put it to a vote. Let's see who believes in saving this company. Who has faith?"

Rockwell turned his eyes slowly to Skip. "I have faith in the market," he intoned. "I vote with Rand."

Letitia stood up. "Well, a vote has been called. All in favor of giving Skip what he's asked for?" She looked around the room and began to count.

Skip noted that Shania and Roberta's daughter were voting with him, as well as at least half of the other younger McCormacks.

Letitia marked down the vote. "And now, all those against?"

Skip looked down at Joseph, who had been tallying the votes. Joseph looked up and shook his head.

Letitia counted out the votes. "Nine, ten, eleven. Well, with the proxies, that's the vote. Eleven for, and eleven against, a tie. I'm afraid a tie means no confidence, Skip."

Skip felt his legs go as he sank into his chair. He heard the laughter and clinking glasses from the other end of the table.

Then suddenly, Jenna jumped up from her seat. "Aunt Letty, aren't you forgetting? *You* didn't vote!"

The room fell silent once more.

Letitia turned and allowed herself a dry cackling laugh. "Why, my dear, you're right. It's the funniest thing! How could I have forgotten my own vote?" She paused for a moment and took a sip of wine.

"Well?" asked Rockwell.

"I'm voting for Skip!" she declared. "That's what Father would have wanted, I'm sure of it!"

The younger McCormacks erupted in a show of celebration. Some of the older ones scowled, muttered, and shook their heads. *Six months and this nut case would be out of a job,* a few of them had already decided.

Shania practically jumped over the table to give Skip a high five. "Listen, I've got some thoughts on how to improve our digital presence," she said, her eyes flashing.

"I want to hear every one of them," Skip promised. The other young members surrounded him, bubbling with ideas.

Joseph let out a huge whoosh of air. He hadn't even been aware of how long he'd been holding his breath.

Jenna leaned in. "You know the biggest joke of all, right?"

Joseph nodded.

"Spending $100 million would have been the *last* thing old

Trader Larry would have wanted. But let Aunt Letty think that!" she said.

Chapter Thirteen

"And then, we sat and watched Letitia start to count up the votes," said Skip, excitedly.

Joseph couldn't help but smile as Skip paused for a moment in his recounting for Gabby and Sam the incredible adventure that was now known as "The Great San Francisco Pyramid Vote." On the way down, the two young people had pestered him for details about what had transpired. Joseph just grinned and said, "I'll let Skip tell you." When they arrived at the office, Skip launched into his story.

And now, as it was reaching its climax, Joseph watched in fascination as Gabby edged closer and closer to the front of her favorite La-Z-Boy, rapt with attention.

"And? And?" Gabby exclaimed.

Sam was more restrained. But his hands were balled into fists, and his eyes were locked on Skip.

"That was it, the vote was tied. I had lost." Skip said.

Gabby slumped back into the recliner so hard it practically fell over on top of her. "Augh!" she exclaimed.

Sam looked on with sympathy. "I told you; she hates to lose."

"But wait, there's more!" Skip said. He was clearly enjoying this moment.

Let him, Joseph thought. *He deserves it.*

Skip recounted how Jenna saved the day and the celebration that followed.

"We won!"

Gabby vaulted out of her chair. "Yes! Go, Aunt Letty!"

Sam nodded. "You, sir, tell a very good story."

"High praise coming from a man who spends most of his days reading one of the greatest stories of all time," said Skip.

"Some see those old stories as ancient history," Sam replied. "But your battle pitting family members against each other would fit right into the Mahabharata, I am sure!"

Joseph stood up and looked out the window. Somehow, humble little Fuller Park didn't seem so bad after spending time in the snake pit of a ritzy San Francisco hotel. "All right team, now comes the hard work."

Skip nodded and gestured to a chart on a screen in front of him. "So, we've got six months, let's get on with it. I've already activated implementation teams and they're moving forward on the identified critical initiatives."

Joseph held up a hand. "That's great! Now you need to visit the prioritized stores and meet each of our managers in person. They need to hear this vision directly from you in their environment. This is how we will build the foundation for the Pyramid brand from the inside out."

Gabby looked at her iPad and set it in front of her. "You know that you'll never get the real picture or honest answers if we just waltz into one of your stores and say, 'Hi! I'm the CEO and I'd like you to tell me how to run my business.'"

Skip thought for a moment. "Of course not. We want to see things as they are."

"The idea is for you and Coach to go in as participant observers," Gabby replied. "In this ethnographic approach, you don't have to disguise your identity, but you still get to see people's *true* behaviors and *authentic* attitudes, rather than a scripted performance."

"It's a combination of art and science," Joseph added. "We'll probably learn as we go, which will allow us to identify where, when, and how we direct our focus."

"Isn't it most important for Skip to let them know that he is doing this for them?" asked Sam. "That this isn't some publicity stunt designed to make him look good?"

Skip gave Joseph a skeptical look. "And how exactly do we do that?"

"I think we have to practice first," Joseph said. "Let's see if we can figure out the best way to approach them *before* we hit the road."

Gabby clapped her hands together. "Role-playing! Yes! Skip, you'll love it!"

"Okay, it sounds like media training," Skip replied. He sounded dubious.

Joseph came around the desk and helped Skip off with his jacket. "First off, no jacket and tie. We want them to see you as a person, not a suit, right?"

Sam leaned in. "You know, when the five Pandava brothers were in exile, they dressed in disguise to infiltrate the King's court. It was quite funny. The great Arjuna pretended to be a eunuch, and Bhima posed as a cook."

"Between those two choices, I think I'd rather be Bhima," Skip said.

"He does have certain traits that you could emulate," Sam went on. "He was a great leader who inspired his armies. He also was said to have the strength of ten thousand elephants."

Skip sighed. "Well, that's quite a lot to live up to."

"There was a general who assaulted Bhima's wife, and then Bhima disguised himself in her silks and waited for the general the next night," Sam said, standing up.

Joseph eyed him. "Is this going to take long?"

Gabby rested her head on her hand. "Once he gets going it's hard to stop him."

Sam's eyes were shining. "I haven't gotten to the good part! The general, Kichaka, tried to attack Bhima, thinking it was his wife, Draupadi. But Bhima rose up and killed him."

"Is that it?" asked Joseph.

"Well, he also ground him up and made him into meatballs, if you want to know the whole story," Sam said.

There was a pause.

"And that's relevant to this how?" asked Gabby.

Sam thought for a minute. "Just be careful when you're in disguise. You might not hear things you like."

"Right," said Joseph. "Let's get this going. Gabby is going to play the part of a cashier and you're going to talk to her."

Skip crossed his arms. "Is this really necessary?"

"When was the last time you shopped for groceries?" asked Joseph.

"Well, I mean, it had to be, um…" Skip said.

Joseph gently shoved Skip by the shoulders. "I thought so. The last thing we need is publicity of you not knowing the price of a gallon of milk or how to talk to one of your workers, like Roberta McCormack and her staff. Right?"

"Right," Skip admitted.

He walked up to Gabby. She reached into her bag and took out a stick of gum.

"What are you doing?" asked Joseph.

"Getting into character," Gabby told him. She put the

gum in her mouth and began chewing loudly. Then she took out her phone and proceeded to scroll through her social feed.

Skip approached her and cleared his throat. Gabby ignored him and continued to look at her phone.

"Excuse me, can I have a word with you?" Skip tried.

"If you're looking for the manager, he's on the second floor, the door next to the bathroom," Gabby said, glued to her phone screen.

Joseph and Skip turned and looked at Sam, who shrugged. "Don't look at me. She's presenting you with a challenge. It's your job to break through."

Skip tried a new tack. "Hey, have you seen the new iPhone? It's pretty amazing."

Gabby slowly turned around. "I wouldn't know," she said flatly.

Skip took his out and showed her. "They've really improved the camera."

Gabby regarded it. "Yeah, that's great. But I can't afford it on the checks I make here. This one was my mom's."

"So, why do you work here?" asked Skip.

"Good question," Gabby replied. "It was either this or fast food. But I didn't like smelling like French fries when I finished work."

"Pardon me!" Sam said in a loud voice. "Are you going to buy something? You're holding up the line, mister!"

He whispered to Skip. "I'm playing the part of an angry customer."

Skip nodded. "I figured that out."

Sam beamed at Gabby. "See? You thought I wouldn't be good at this!"

"Stay in character!" Gabby hissed.

Joseph stepped in. "Okay, let's stop there. I think there's a lot to work with already."

Gabby's face fell. "But I didn't even get a chance to ring him up."

Joseph rolled his eyes. "We'll do it again, I promise." He checked his notepad, which was filled with scribbled notes. "How did that make you feel when Gabby ignored you?" he asked Skip.

"Irritated. Mad. Unappreciated." Skip said.

Joseph nodded. "But you could understand her lack of enthusiasm?"

"She doesn't see any future and probably feels pretty unappreciated herself," Skip offered.

Sam smiled. "So, what can we do to make her feel *more* appreciated?"

Joseph drew Skip's attention to his computer screen. "Here's a prioritized list of ideas we can implement to make our employees *want* to come to work, instead of *having* to come to work."

Skip looked at the list. "I like it. We're definitely upping the base pay plus giving them schedule flexibility. But, helping them out with college tuition…?"

"More and more businesses are doing this, and it's proven to be a winner," Joseph said. "For now, we can focus on other experiential benefits, like giving them more break time and consider this when the time is right."

"And a break room that doesn't smell like dirty socks," suggested Gabby.

Joseph stood up. "Let's revisit that scene. You saw how aggravated Sam was?"

"He was very aggravated," Skip admitted.

Sam jumped in. "Aggravation! That was exactly what I was

going for! I took an acting class for fun, and I remember the drama teacher telling us to use something from our own lives when we need to find a way to play an emotion. So, I remembered this time when I was shopping for groceries in Chicago and this woman in front of me—"

"I think my cashier was a lot harder to play than your customer," Gabby interrupted. "Nobody said anything about *my* performance."

"Not everything is a competition, dearest," Sam said.

Joseph rubbed his temples. "Guys! This isn't about you! What I was getting at was that this was a perfect opportunity for Skip to talk to one of his customers."

"Maybe I could commiserate with them," Skip said. "See what it was about the experience of shopping at Pyramid that made them so unhappy."

Joseph gave a tight smile. "That's the idea."

For the rest of the afternoon, Gabby, Sam, and Joseph took turns playing different roles. Joseph played a supplier of bathing suits who was thinking of taking his line to another big-box retailer. Sam played a customer who was shopping at Pyramid out of habit but was starting to buy his goods online more often after finding so few of his needs were met at Pyramid today. And Gabby played a manager who blamed everyone and everything but herself for the problems her store was having: lazy employees, shoplifting customers, high prices, damaged products, faulty stocking, and a bad location.

As the day wore on, Skip found himself more and more using the expertise that each of the team brought to the table: Sam's empathy and deep connection with people's needs; Gabby's ability to analyze and reflect on how best to communicate with those people to let them know they were being heard; and Joseph's ability to keep them focused on one goal—finding the best to way to spend the $100 million budget to convince and convert all three stakeholders—guests, employees, and suppliers.

It was getting dark. They had been at this for six hours. Joseph stretched. His notepad was now filled with ideas and dozens of ways to help improve Pyramid's stores. "Good work, everybody. I think we deserve a little rest."

"This was incredibly helpful. I can't thank you enough," Skip told them.

"Don't thank us yet," Joseph said. "We're just starting."

Skip looked at the three of them. "You mean…"

"Same time tomorrow," Joseph grinned.

"I think we should bring props!" Sam declared. "Or at least a few hats!"

Gabby looked at him out of the corner of her eye. "I don't need that stuff. All I need is more gum."

Sam groaned.

"Admit it! My cashier was the *best*!" Gabby giggled, hugging him.

As Joseph packed up, Skip leaned in. "She really does hate to lose, doesn't she?"

Joseph looked right at Skip. He wasn't smiling. "She's not the only one."

Chapter Fourteen

Skip cursed under his breath as he struggled with the zipper on the shiny new winter coat he'd just been handed by Joseph. "Cheap knockoff crap," he muttered.

"Hey! That's your merchandise you're talking about!" laughed Joseph, as he slipped his on. "When I was a kid, I would have killed for a parka this warm!"

Skip regarded Joseph and marveled at the transformation. Gone were the immaculate suits and fitted shirts. Here was Joseph in Pyramid's house brand jeans and patterned sweater. "I think I have a new slogan for those pants," Skip cracked. "Tired of looking like a man on his way up? Our 'Dad Jeans' will give you that 'fell asleep in front of the TV' look that drives women wild."

"We can test market it when we get to the store," Joseph responded dryly, as he hopped into the rented SUV.

As Skip jumped into the front passenger seat he turned to Joseph. "You sure this thing has four-wheel drive? Not sure about those roads."

"I doubt they're allowed to sell anything but four-wheel

drive up here in Buffalo," Joseph said. "Come on, man! You act like you haven't seen snow like this in Chicago."

He put the car in drive, and the GPS kicked in, starting their journey.

"Not like this," Skip replied, eyeing the four-foot-high snow drifts along the side of the road. He grimaced as the car slipped a few feet. "Leave it to Trader Larry to open the first Pyramid store in East Buffalo."

"I'm guessing he got a good deal on the lot, and the mayor's office back then was aggressively soliciting businesses," Joseph informed him.

"Tell me again why we're starting here—and in February," Skip asked.

"Symbolism," Joseph said. "It's one of the worst performing stores in the area and the oldest. If we can get this one going, it'll really say something."

They slowly made their way up the main drag, passing the bleak signs of closed stores and darkened fast-food joints. Joseph carefully turned into a large, mostly deserted parking lot. In front of them was the dilapidated frontage of a once-proud Pyramid anchor store. Some of the windows still had Christmas decorations in them. The other ones had what looked like a half-hearted attempt at a Valentine's Day display.

The two men exchanged glances. This was *not* where either of them wanted to be on Valentine's Day. But they both knew it was where they needed to be. They emerged from the car into the freezing Buffalo air and made for the entrance.

"Big surprise, the automatic doors don't work," said Skip, after standing in front of them for a few seconds.

Joseph pushed the door open. "That should be our biggest problem."

They walked in and approached an older woman in a bright

blue vest, who was deep in her copy of whatever tabloid she'd grabbed from the stand by the cashier. She didn't even look up.

Skip slapped a smile on his face. "Excuse me, ma'am?"

The woman wearily lifted her head. "Yeah?"

"We're looking for men's socks," Skip said.

The woman sighed. "Yeah. I dunno. Maybe try the men's department. Second floor."

"Thanks so much!" Skip said as they walked on ahead.

The woman resumed her reading.

Joseph counted a handful of shoppers in the store. A couple of families wandered around looking like they needed help but couldn't find anyone who worked there. He also saw a man shuffling toward the back of the store who looked like he hadn't had a bath in months.

They found the escalator. Skip regarded it with resignation. "Why am I not surprised it's broken?"

They trudged up "the stairs" and found themselves in a dark, dirty warren of rows filled with merchandise. There seemed to be no order to how the products were laid out on the shelves.

Joseph couldn't help but smile. "Well, I didn't expect to find a volleyball in women's underwear. That's kind of interesting."

"You can smile. You're not the one who's losing his job in five months," said Skip. He had thought the month they had spent working on the strategies and tactics to build trust had been time well spent, but now he wasn't too sure.

They made their way through the piles of unfolded sweaters and pants and found a mostly empty rack of socks. Nearby was a section marked "Winter Coats" with one lonely hooded jacket hanging there.

"Looks like they sold out on their stock," Skip mused.

Joseph checked the label on the coat. "Or they never got the stock in. This is from last year." He looked around. "Now, *that* they have plenty of..."

Skip followed his gaze and saw a rack of gauzy, brightly colored Hawaiian shirts. There were dozens of them. He took out his phone and snapped a photo.

"What do you think you're doing?" demanded a rough voice.

Skip turned around and saw a ruddy-faced man in his fifties. The man had a gray brush cut and bristling eyebrows. He looked like every PE teacher Skip ever hated. "I'm just taking a few photos if you don't mind," he told him.

The man pushed in, so he was almost right on top of Skip. "Not allowed. Delete those photos. *Now.*"

"Yeah, I don't think so," responded Skip and turned away.

The man grabbed Skip by the arm. "I ain't fooling around, you little dirtbag."

Joseph saw this escalating and stepped in. "May I ask your position here?"

The man turned and saw Joseph for the first time. "My *position*?" he asked. "You want to know my position? Screw you, that's my position."

Skip pulled his arm back. "I need to speak to the manager."

The crew-cut man cocked his head to one side. "I bet you do, sweetheart."

"Right now," Skip said sternly.

The man stuck his face so close to Skip he could count the spider veins on his nose. "You're talking to him. *I'm* the manager."

Skip kept his voice level low. "Pleased to meet you. I'm Skip Collinsworth, the CEO of Pyramid."

The man laughed. "And I'm the tooth fairy."

Joseph took his phone out and turned the screen to the man. "Actually, he's telling the truth."

The man peered at the screen. On it was a photo of Skip from a *Business Insider* profile Pyramid's publicity department wrote, with the headline, "Pyramid CEO to tour stores, vows to bring the brand back to its glory days."

The man looked back and forth from the screen to Skip. Then, as the information sunk in, he backed away. His mouth was working, but no words were coming out. He suddenly had the face of someone who just realized he couldn't remember his soon-to-be wife's name at the altar at his wedding.

Skip brushed himself off. "So, you were saying, I believe, that you were the tooth fairy?"

The man put out a grimy paw. "Well, er, no. I'm, uh, actually, Mr. Collinsworth, I'm Mel Cooley, the night manager. Our head manager is out today."

"So, you're minding the store, as it were," Joseph said.

"I mean, I wouldn't say that. I just—you gotta forgive me, Mr. Collinsworth. I was looking out for your property if you see what I mean. You know, there are a lot of homeless people who make themselves at home here, and I just thought, uh..."

Joseph took pity on the flailing Mr. Cooley. "We know all about the homeless," he said. "We saw quite a few of them wandering around downstairs."

Mel snapped into action. He grabbed a phone off the wall. "We'll take care of that, don't you worry."

He spoke into the receiver. "Security. Security." There was no sound coming through the speakers. He sheepishly hung up the phone.

"How long has that been broken?" asked Skip.

"Now that's a question for Mr. Davis. He's the head manager. I'm just the night manager. I don't know nothin."

"At least perhaps you could tell me about those," Skip said, pointing to the display of gaudy aloha-style shirts. "Big sellers, are they?"

Mel grimaced. "Yeah, I dunno about that. They're not really moving. Not a lot of call for them in Buffalo, if you know what I mean."

Skip nodded. He looked around the sorry mess of a store that he needed to clean up in the next few months. "I've seen enough," he said to Joseph. "Time for the next step."

Joseph nodded. They headed out. The next few hours would be used to ensure teams were debriefed and focused on the most critical problems and as soon as possible.

As they started to leave, Mel called after them. "No hard feelings, right, boss? I was just doing my job."

Skip thought for a minute. "Oh, your job. Yes, about that."

Joseph pulled him aside. "Skip, as good as it would feel to fire the guy, it would be terrible if it got out. Morale in the company is low enough. Remember, we're trying to get these people to perform better. The guy's been beaten down and ignored his whole life."

Skip turned to Mel. "Don't worry."

Mel sighed with relief. "So, I'm not fired?"

"Let's just say you're on notice," suggested Skip.

"Got it!" said Mel, saluting.

Skip returned the salute, feeling a little ridiculous. But Joseph was onto something. Maybe, just maybe, he could get the people in the stores fired up if they were just treated right.

Chapter Fifteen

Skip rubbed his eyes and yawned. He never thought there would be a day when he would be so glad to return to HQ. But after the two months he and Joseph had put in on the road, it was nice to be home.

Joseph had somehow arranged a schedule that allowed them to see a hundred stores in eight weeks, including spending time with employees and even hearing from customers. Thanks to Joseph, they made their way down from Buffalo to stores in the Rust Belt, followed by stores in the Deep South. Working their way around Texas, the best thing Skip could say was that he had become a connoisseur of barbecue, tasting all of its varieties as they stopped in one small restaurant after another.

Back at headquarters, Skip watched as twenty-five chairs were being brought into the biggest room they had in the old place. He turned to Joseph and shook his head. "Getting every regional manager to come to a meeting in Illinois and setting everything up in such a short time, It's nothing short of a miracle."

"Don't thank me," Joseph said. "Those two ladies put it all together." He pointed at Gabby and Skip's executive assistant, Thelma, who had been organizing this meeting for weeks. They were flying from one part of the room to another, making sure there were enough pastries and bear claws, and checking to see when the coffee would be ready. They looked like they were having the time of their lives.

Skip grabbed the two of them. "Hey, ladies! This is fantastic! I don't know how you did it."

Gabby impulsively gave Skip a hug. "Hey! Welcome back, General! It's just logistics and I had a ton of help from Thelma and other Pyramid team members."

Something then caught Gabby's eye. "Excuse me, I need to make sure each chair has an agenda!"

Joseph scanned his phone. A smile crossed his face. "Yes!"

Skip looked over. "Earnings report look good?" he asked hopefully.

Joseph put his phone back in his pocket. No reason for Skip to see that part. "Yeah, well, you know, it takes a while to see those kinds of concrete results. But some of the changes we're making seem to be doing the job."

Skip checked his watch. "Looks like it's showtime."

Joseph nodded. Sam was there, shepherding the assembled group of Pyramid's regional leaders. There was something calming about Sam. As he touched a shoulder here or smiled at someone there, he seemed to radiate a sense that they were here for more than just a pep talk. Rather, these regional leaders were here to help solve the problems that each one faced day after day as they tried to keep their stores going.

Skip could see their faces light up when they saw the pastry table, and most of them grabbed some goodies and a cup of coffee before finding a seat. After a few minutes, Skip moved to the podium. He raised his hands and the room fell silent.

"Most of you know me by now," Skip began. "But for the few of you I haven't had the pleasure to meet yet, I'm Skip

Collinsworth, CEO of Pyramid, and I want to welcome you to our headquarters."

A tall, gangly man with graying sideburns raised his hand. Skip steeled himself for whatever was going to come out of the man's mouth.

"My name's Morgan, Jim Morgan," the man said in the clipped accent of a native New Englander. "And I just wanted to say thanks for having us here. The last time I was invited was when old Trader Larry was still in charge."

There were murmurs of assent from the older men scattered around the room.

Skip grinned. "I think you'll notice that there's a difference between your last time and this one. I'm guessing when Trader Larry brought you here, he talked and you listened."

There was knowing laughter.

"Well," Skip continued. "Today, I'm here to let *you* talk and *I'm* going to listen." He could see nodding from most of the assembled managers.

Jim Morgan spoke up. "I never heard that once from any of the McCormacks!"

That got applause.

Skip gave a small bow. "Okay, let's get started. How are things looking in your stores?"

A woman stood up. She was in her late forties. "Sheila Jacobs, Southeast Region. We're really happy that you've given us the resources to finally remodel our stores. And I like that there's even a discretionary budget that lets us choose the local markets where we should advertise."

More nodding heads.

Sheila went on. "But there's still a supply issue. I haven't gotten half the Easter baskets and stuffed animals I need. We should have gotten them yesterday. It's already a little late, and

I'm afraid we'll be stuck with inventory when Easter's come and gone."

Skip turned to Joseph. "We hear you. Is this affecting anyone else's region?" asked Joseph.

A few hands went up, calling out their areas. He marked them down on a sheet.

"Anyone sitting on too much inventory? We're trying to figure out if we can help each other?"

A man in the back yelled out. "I got a warehouse full of pink bunnies! Happy to send half of them your way, Sheila!"

There was a lot of chatter after that. Thelma hurried over to get the man's information.

Others mentioned where they were short, and the room descended into horse trading, as the managers began helping one another.

Skip clapped his hands to quiet things down. "Great start, guys! But let's get this organized. We'll put up a form on the website, and you can communicate better that way."

"You mean the one that crashes every time I try to log in?" groused a short, bald man with a tan and a toothpick in his mouth.

"We're working on that," Joseph said. "Until our website is fixed, we've set up a separate secure portal just for inter-managerial communications. The address is on the sheet in front of you."

Skip knew that the harder questions were coming. He had to prime the pump, or they'd never get asked. "So, how's morale with your employees?"

A woman with bleached blonde hair in a pink pantsuit waved her hand. "Christie Ellis, Upper Midwest Region."

Skip indicated for her to go on.

"I can say that everyone loves our new flexible schedule, the new break room, and the free coffee and donuts in there has been a big hit," Christie said. "But the truth is that the unions are still pushing us hard on pay. It's causing a lot of bad feelings. They see money being spent on making the stores look good, but none of it is going into their pockets."

The room had gone silent.

"Is that something everyone is seeing?" Skip asked.

There was a feeling of discomfort in the room. Clearly, a nerve had been hit.

"Well, I have good news for you. We've been in negotiations with the union."

There was practically a gasp from the assembled managers.

Skip laughed. "I know, top management talking to union reps? Unheard of at Pyramid, right? Well, we've got to get *everyone* on board if this is going to work. So, I'm going to give you all a little scoop on what we've been working on and keeping under our hats. Tomorrow, Pyramid is going to announce a new initiative called 'Workers Trust,' a tiered system with base pay at $18 an hour, going up to $26 for those with tenure. And we will pay tuition for any of our employees going to community college. This is what the union is going to bring to your employees. We want them to know we care about them and their livelihoods."

There were whoops and applause around the room. Skip knew that these managers would welcome anything that would retain their employees and make them happy.

Skip spoke over the burble of excited voices. "Guys! Guys! This is why I brought you here. Because when we're together we can solve anything. We may represent different regions, but we all want the same thing—for Pyramid to succeed."

A woman with long black hair stood up. Skip recognized her immediately as Gina Estevez, who was the regional manager for

Texas. There were so many stores in Texas, alone, that it had its own rep.

"While we're asking for things, this is something I've been asking for years."

"Go ahead, Gina," Skip said. She was one of the most powerful voices in the room and needed no introduction.

"Our stores in Texas are located in communities that have a sizable Latino population. Shouldn't we finally have bilingual signage throughout our businesses?"

From the corner, a voice yelled, "Florida and surrounding states agree!"

Then another, "California says, *Ya es hora!*"

Skip remembered his high school Spanish. "For those who don't know, that means, 'It's about time!'"

Joseph pointed to the pages that the managers had been given. Skip glanced at the sheet and then turned back to the woman from Texas. "Gina, if you turn to page three, you'll see that's already on our list. That signage should be in your stores by next week."

Gina raised her fist and beamed. "Nice!"

Joseph turned to Gabby and Sam, who were standing behind him. Gabby leaned in. "It's going great, right?"

Joseph nodded. This was the good side of groupthink. When the room is filled with promises, it felt like they could accomplish anything. But break a few of those promises and things could change quickly. He knew that trust is fragile, and if you lose it, it can be very hard to get it back.

A man whose physique said he'd enjoyed his share of beers and burgers slowly rose to his feet. His face was lined with wrinkles, and his hair and beard were white making him look like a cross between Santa Claus and a Biblical prophet. No one had to be told who he was, least of all Skip. His name was Derek

Passerell, and he had been with Pyramid practically from the beginning. The room grew silent, and all eyes were on the old man.

He said nothing at first, regarding Skip with what seemed to be bemusement. Finally, he spoke. "So, Mr. Collinsworth. You've certainly brought a lot of wonderful ideas to this meeting. And like all my friends here, I'm not used to being listened to."

Skip came forward from behind the podium. "Go on, Mr. Passerell. I'm still listening."

"Let me ask you a question, then," Derek said. "How long have you been with this company?"

Skip eyed Joseph, worried where this might be going. "A little over a year."

Derek's eyes narrowed. "Well, you see, here's the thing. I've been with Pyramid for *fifty years.* I started as a stock boy when I was in high school. Old man McCormack saw something in me and pulled me along, and now look at me! The 'grand old man' of the company."

"An American success story if I ever heard one," Skip said.

Derek waved him off. "Oh, bull. I been here because there's nothing else I know how to do. But that's not my point. My point is that in six months, I'll still be here. Well, where will you be? We're not stupid, Mr. Skip Collinsworth. You may think we're simple folks, but we read *The Wall Street Journal* just like you do. We know you're on borrowed time. If you don't make a go of this, you'll be gone after the next earnings come in. And so will all your pretty promises." He turned to his fellow managers, waving the paper. "All of this goes away if young Mr. Collinsworth here can't produce. Just remember that."

Skip folded his arms. "You are absolutely right, Mr. Passerell. Except for one detail: I never thought any of you were simple. You are smart, hard-working people who've had to overcome a lot to get where you are. And for most of the last decade, you had to fight every inch of the way, as one CEO after another knocked the legs out from under you. This time you have a CEO who's fighting for you. And, I hope, fighting *with* you."

Skip held his eyes onto the unwavering gaze of the old man. "Yes, I'll be gone if we don't get our earnings up. I'm asking you to help me do that." And then looking at all the regional leaders, "I'm *trusting* you. Because the alternative, as Mr. Passerell here knows full well, is that when I go, the next CEO will be a bean counter who will enjoy nothing more than cutting wages, ignoring the union, and lopping off our suppliers at the knees."

"Is that what you want? Is that what you think you want to value? Is that the company you want to work for? If you want change, if you want Pyramid to be not only what it was when Trader Larry led it, but what it can be in the future, I need you to help me make it happen. What do you say?"

Drew stroked his beard. "Well, I suppose you know I've already been approached by Mr. Rand Swigert to wait for a few months and not do anything until he takes over."

Gabby grabbed Joseph's arm and squeezed.

"I'm sure he made you quite an offer," Skip said, grimly.

"Yep. His retirement package was, let's just say it was generous. Any of the rest of you hear from this Swigert?"

A dozen hands went up, including, sheepishly, Gina Estevez.

Joseph stepped forward. "So, was that the plan? Agree to everything Skip said and then sit on your hands until the clock ran out?"

"Look," Gina said. "He made a pretty good case. If the company is going to go down, why go down with it? He's offering us a lot of money."

"An awfully tempting offer, it's true," smiled the old man. "But then again, I've been at Pyramid my whole working life.

I've given both my heart and soul to this company." He looked at Skip for what seemed like an eternity, then he made his pronouncement. "We're talking about trust here. What reason do we have to trust that greasy son of a gun Swigert? He can screw you or me just like he's going to do it to the unions and our suppliers." He put out his hand. "I like you, Mr. Collinsworth. And what's more, I *do* trust you."

As they shook hands, he announced to his fellow managers, "I say we do everything we can to help this young feller!"

As the room broke out in cheers, Joseph looked down at his arm, where Gabby had been gripping it. "That's going to leave a bruise," he told her.

"Who cares?" she whooped, as Sam hugged her, and then Joseph. "We won!"

Joseph looked at his two young colleagues and had to admit to himself, he'd never had so much fun in his life.

Chapter Sixteen

As Joseph Chandler rode down the elevator from his comfortable executive suite in the Courtyard Hotel, he took stock of the last few days. The Courtyard might not be the Ritz-Carlton, but it was a well-appointed place in the heart of downtown Phoenix, chosen because it was within a few blocks of the largest Pyramid store in Arizona. Afterall, you didn't want to walk too long outside in the heat of an Arizona April.

He and Skip had toured the store yesterday, and Joseph marveled at what could be accomplished in just four months. Well-stocked shelves, with items where they should be, and prices clearly marked. Fresh, new displays welcomed customers to the bargains and values that they'd always looked for at a Pyramid store. Joseph had made sure to chat with as many employees as he could, from the ones who stocked the shelves to the cashiers and security guards. It felt a lot different from the shabby, dim stores they had been seeing in the first months of this amazing voyage.

Sure, they'd bumped heads with a few managers, who balked at having to do things a new way. These men had taken it easy for years, secure in the knowledge that no one was looking over their shoulders. But there were now eager, young talent in the company more than happy to take over from the dead weight. They were there because they trusted Skip, knowing that they had a once-in-a-lifetime opportunity to be part of bringing a once-great brand back to life.

And most importantly, there were the customers. New marketing and sales programs were already bringing people back into the stores in droves. But would it be enough?

The doors to the elevator opened, and Joseph strode through the lobby to The Bistro, the hotel restaurant where he was meeting Skip for breakfast. He walked into the sleek, light-filled café and found Skip in the back, sitting hunched over at a table, with nothing but a cup of coffee in front of him.

"Good morning, Skipper!" Joseph exclaimed. "That's no way to start the day! You need your carbs, bud."

Skip looked up and shook his head. Joseph hadn't seen him like this since they'd set off on this adventure together. But he knew enough to expect it. At some point, the reality of what they were trying to do would sneak in.

"Well, I'm thinking about a scone and maybe some granola. You sure you don't want anything?"

Skip waved him off.

"Hey, what happened to the man who was single-handedly going to save one of America's most beloved brands?"

"Let's save the happy talk for the workers," Skip snapped.

Joseph sat down. "So, what's this all about?"

"What's this all about?" Skip repeated. "It's about the fact that our sales numbers aren't showing the kind of growth we need. The March report just came out and it's, well, it's better than we'd hoped, but—"

Joseph put a finger to his lips. A waiter came to take his

order. "I think I'll have your signature breakfast sandwich and a latte."

"Very good, sir," the waiter replied, turning to Skip. "And for you, sir?"

Before Skip could answer, Joseph said, "He'll have the same."

The waiter turned and left.

Then Joseph saw what had thrown Skip into his funk. He reached over and grabbed Skip's iPad and saw the main story on the *Forbes* digital homepage. "So, this is it, huh?" he asked.

There was a photoshopped picture of Skip, in painter's pants, holding a brush. The headline read, "Return of a Dynasty or Pyramid Scheme? Pyramid's new CEO's got plans. But is it real, or just a thin coat of new paint? Behind Skip Collinsworth's $100 million gamble to save his job."

Joseph sighed. "You don't take it seriously, do you?"

Skip nodded. "Why shouldn't I? They have quotes from some of the smartest minds in retail telling me how this can't be done."

"Skip, these guys are old school," said Joseph. "What they're really saying is, 'It's never been done before.'"

Skip gave a dry laugh. "Yeah, we know how Wall Street loves untried things."

Joseph took out his phone and scrolled through a series of emails. "Yeah, but we're getting results. Your margins are growing every month."

"True," Skip admitted. "I mean if I had a few years maybe, but six months? I must have been crazy."

Joseph shook his head. "I'm telling you; we just need to let things work. There are a few more pieces of the puzzle that need to be fixed, and I think we're going to pull this off."

"What makes me feel especially bad is that you've spent

your entire sabbatical running around the country sleeping in hotel rooms, instead of spending time with your family," Skip rejoined.

The food arrived and Joseph took a bite of his sandwich. He wiped his mouth with a napkin. "What? And miss the breakfast sandwich at the Courtyard Hotel? I hear people travel like a few blocks just to have this."

Skip allowed himself a small smile.

"Don't worry about me," Joseph continued. "I needed this as much as you did. People like those so-called experts *Forbes* pulled quotes from aren't living out here. They're sitting behind desks in comfy, tenured positions, or they're experts trapped in legacy category paradigms." He picked up the iPad and flipped through the pages. "Look at this guy. 'Companies don't need consultants at the top, with gimmicks and slogans. They need finance people. People who understand the financial market. Who know how to cut costs.'"

Skip shrugged. "What if he's right?"

Joseph tilted his head to one side. "Skip, buddy, who is the quote from? Fred Silversmith."

Skip thought for a minute. "Why is that name familiar?"

"It should be," Joseph said, "Remember Silversmith and Swigert? He's Rand's ex-business partner!"

Skip looked at his plate. "Maybe I am a little hungry."

"And this one? A source from within the company told us that there was mounting discontent among the district managers, who don't like being lectured to or told how to do their job by some young kid who's never run anything in his life."

Skip swallowed and took a gulp of coffee. "Yeah, that one I mean, if it's true."

"Wake up!" Joseph told him. "An *unnamed* source from

'within the company?' Who does that sound like? To me, it has Rand Swigert's and Rockwell McCormack's fingerprints all over it."

Skip looked at the quote. "Yeah, I see what you mean."

Joseph finished his sandwich and let Skip think for a minute. "So, Mister CEO, what does that tell you? I mean someone went to an awful lot of trouble to plant that article."

"It means they're running scared," Skip said, an honest smile breaking out on his face.

"That's what I think, too," Joseph told him. "We've got a friendly interviewer from *Business Insider* meeting us at our next stop. Fight fire with fire, right?"

Skip drained his coffee. "I guess so. Hey, thanks for the pep talk."

Joseph knew this wasn't enough. There was a chirp from his phone. He glanced down at the text on his screen. *Perfect timing!* he thought. His little surprise had arrived.

Skip brushed the crumbs off his polo shirt. "So, what's on the agenda for today?"

"Oh, I thought you could use a little distraction, what with you working so hard these past months," Joseph said.

"A little too hot for golf, wouldn't you say?" said Skip.

"That wasn't what I was thinking," Joseph replied.

All of a sudden, a familiar voice broke the conversation. "Excuse me, but is this seat taken?"

Skip looked up to see Jenna holding a tray. He looked back at Joseph, who was beaming. "You set this up, didn't you?"

"She didn't need much convincing," Joseph said, as he got up from the table. "You can have my seat. I was just leaving."

Jenna kissed Joseph on the cheek. "You're the best. See you at dinner?"

Joseph looked back at Skip, who was gazing at his beautiful

wife. "Well, let's play that by ear. Just don't keep him up too late!" Joseph headed out into the lobby, leaving the happy couple to themselves. He pressed a button on his phone and made a call.

"Hello?" he heard Dionne Chandler reply.

"Well, your plan was perfect," he said. "It was just what the doctor ordered."

The voice on the other end was clearly pleased with herself. "So, what do you say, dear?"

Joseph sighed. "Always listen to your wife."

"You better remember that!" she said.

Joseph suddenly heard yelling in the background.

"Boys! Boys! Who wants to speak to Daddy?" said Dionne.

Chapter Seventeen

As their Uber glided through the sun-dappled streets of downtown San Mateo, California, Joseph gazed out the tinted windows and understood why so many tech companies had chosen to make their home here. A stone's throw from San Francisco, it had all the amenities of a big city but still the feel of a smaller town. And once the big players like YouTube and Roblox had moved their corporate headquarters here, it was like eating at the cool kids' table in middle school. If you wanted to consider yourself a player, you had to be here.

Skip was flipping through pages on his iPad, navigating through the confusing menus and complicated order forms some overpaid tech "geniuses,"as Skip called them, had thrown together to make Pyramid's website.

He turned to Joseph. "So, they don't know we're coming?"

"Not as far as I know," Joseph said. "The only ones who might tell them are Rand and Rockwell, but they weren't informed of our little visit."

Skip had a tight, little smile on his face. "That's good. Perfect."

The Uber came to a stop in front of a glass and steel skyscraper at 400 S. El Camino Real, and Joseph and Skip got out of the car and looked up at one of the many glass towers that lined this part of town. Pyramid Online Express (or POE, as the "geniuses" had branded it, complete with a Raven mascot for some reason) took residence on the second floor of the building, stretching across vast amounts of expensive office space.

Skip approached the welcome desk in the lobby and greeted the willowy blonde receptionist with a smile.

She looked up at him, unimpressed. "Good morning. Who are you here to see?"

"Paul Chaplin," Skip said, pleasantly. "But no need to introduce us. We'll see ourselves up." He looked at the young woman's name tag, "Piper."

Piper gave Skip a look that was a cross between pity and condescension. "I'm afraid that's impossible. I need to see—"

"*I* need to see Mr. Chaplin. Now." Skip added a little steel to his voice.

"And you are?" demanded Piper.

Skip took out his pass and showed it to her. Joseph had made sure that the home office had secured them visitors' passes before they got there. He hadn't specified the names or when they were coming.

"Skip Collinsworth, CEO of Pyramid Stores," Skip informed her.

Piper choked a little. "Oh! Er, right! I thought you looked familiar. You know, from the magazine covers."

A mountain of a security guard in a black T-shirt and shades wandered over. He rested a cartoonishly big arm on the desk. "Everything okay over here, Piper?"

She nodded. "It's all good, Bela. This is our CEO, Mr. Collinsworth."

Bela's face broke out into a grin. "Well! Welcome to San Mateo, sir. Glad to have you here."

"Thanks," Skip said. "We need to get going."

Bela turned to Joseph. "I like his style. You know my mama worked at Pyramid for thirty years. I wish she was here to see this."

"I'm so sorry to hear she's gone," Joseph said. "When did she pass?"

"Oh, she's not dead," Bela assured him. "She just moved down to So-Cal to live with my sister."

"Got it," said Joseph, as he followed Skip through the sliding glass partitions that opened with a whoosh as their ID cards were read.

Skip turned back to Piper, who had picked up her phone. "Remember, do not announce us. This is a surprise."

Piper carefully put the receiver down. "Right. Sorry. Force of habit."

The elevator doors closed, and they were taken to the second floor, where Skip was greeted with a Nerf dart flying directly at his face. He ducked as it hit the back of the elevator.

A genial-looking twenty-something emerged from behind a giant potted plant holding a bright blue Nerf gun. "Oh, sorry, dude! My bad!"

There was a "thwack!" and a dart whizzed by the young man's face. "Incoming!" he yelled and ran off.

There were shouts and gleeful trash-talking throughout the large, modern office space. Everywhere you looked there were Eames chairs and other mid-century furniture.

Joseph pointed to a desk. "That's a Herman Miller. That desk, alone, costs $4,000."

"Spare no expense, I guess, when it's other people's money," Skip said, as they wandered further into the office area.

It was an open space, with tables set up with rows of top-of-the-line Apple products lined up like little soldiers.

As they walked down the hallway, along the wall were glassed-in rooms, usually used for conferences. But here, one had a ping-pong table, another had a massage table, and a third had a Zen Garden.

"I mean, all this stuff would be great if they were making money," admitted Joseph.

"I've met a few of these tech bros," Skip said. "They spend VC money like it's water."

As they turned a corner, they saw a gaggle of guys sitting around throwing wadded paper toward a garbage can. No one, it seemed, was working.

There was a larger space marked off with sliding glass doors. Behind it was a huge desk, with four monitors on it. Ambient music blared out of Bluetooth speakers. Next to the desk was a yoga mat. On the mat was a bare-chested man who, like the others, appeared to be in his twenties. His butt was in the air, in the downward dog pose.

Skip spoke to the man's rear end. "You wouldn't be Paul Chaplin, would you?"

The young man did not get up. He moved into another pose. "Who wants to know?"

Skip knelt down and looked the young man dead in the eyes. "The CEO of Pyramid Stores, that's who."

Paul slowly got up out of his pose and stretched. He moved over and turned off the music. "So, you're the big man with the plan, huh?"

"And you're the dude with the attitude," said Joseph, shaking his head disdainfully.

Skip turned and looked at him.

"That's the title of the article on him in *Wired,*" Joseph explained. "I didn't come up with it."

"Hey, it's all good," Paul said, pulling on a cashmere shirt. "I mean, we're cool, right?"

Skip pulled up an Aeron chair and took a seat behind the desk.

"Whoa, power move," chuckled Paul. "You showing me you're the alpha dog?"

"Let's cut the crap," Skip said. "I know you got your MBA from Wharton. What's your game?"

Paul looked hurt. "Whoa, slow down. You're bringing some real nasty East Coast vibes into my space."

Skip took out his iPad. "Paul, you've had this site up for a year now. It's still got more bugs than the American Embassy in Moscow. What gives?"

Paul shrugged. "Hey man, these things take time. We have more traffic than we can handle. Can I help it if we created a site with this much heat?"

"As a matter of fact," Joseph said. "Your traffic has been consistently going down every month. Isn't that so?"

Paul looked at Joseph as if seeing him for the first time. "Who is this suit? What's *his* game?"

"He's a consultant who's been helping me restructure Pyramid. His name is Joseph Chandler."

"A *consultant*?" Paul said, as if it was the filthiest thing you could call someone. "Oh, I get it, a rent-a-suit."

"Not exactly," Joseph said, trying to keep his cool.

"I bet you're a professor of business somewhere, right?" said Paul. "I bet you've never even created a startup. Have you?"

Joseph picked up Skip's iPad. "You don't have to be a chef to know if the food is lousy at a restaurant."

"Oh, wow! So original!" said Paul with a smirk. "Okay, let me ask you something. You know what the KPIs are for e-comm?"

Skip paused. He knew the key performance indicators for retail, but e-commerce was its own beast. He shook his head.

"Yeah, I didn't think so," Paul said. "Look, why don't you go back to the dark ages of brick and mortar and leave the visionary stuff to guys like me? We're getting it done."

Skip shook his head. "The problem is, you're *not* getting it done."

"These things take time," Paul told him. He grabbed a protein bar from his desk and bit off a piece. "And I happen to know when you don't make your numbers in a month you'll be gone. And you don't know jack about the digital ecosystem and how quickly it's evolving, so I guess you're stuck with me."

Skip folded his arms. "You know Paul, we see you," he began. "You can't snow us with that 'visionary' crap. You didn't create anything. You're only here because you were Rand Swigert's son's roommate at Brown. He's the one who put you in, isn't that so?"

Paul stopped chewing. "Yeah, so what? There's no way you two dudes are going to find anyone to staff this site in six months, let alone one."

"You know," Joseph told him. "You were right about us not knowing this space. But you know who does?"

Paul rolled his eyes. "Who?"

Joseph was looking over Paul's shoulder at the young woman who'd just entered the room.

Skip sat bolt upright at the desk. He knew that nose piercing.

"You were asking about the KPIs for e-commerce?" Shania McCormack said. "Let's see, there's CVRs, you know, conversion rate benchmarks. There's AOVs, average order value benchmarks. There's also bounce rate and engagement. Do you want me to continue?"

Paul looked dismayed.

"And I've been looking at *your* site's CVRs, AOVs, bounce rate, and engagement, and you know what?" Shania said. "They *suck.*"

Paul turned pale. "Who is she?"

"May I present Shania McCormack, our new Chief Digital Officer at Pyramid," Joseph said. "I guess you might say she's your new boss, *dude.*"

Skip leaped up and came over to Shania. "Yes! Joseph didn't tell me!"

Shania smirked. "That's on me. I told him not to. I like surprises as much as you do."

A crowd of scruffy young men had gathered at the door, drawn to the commotion.

Shania turned to the assemblage of man-children. "So, here's the deal. You want to code, you want to work, you want to stay here until we get this site right? Then stick around. Otherwise, take your things and turn in your pass card at the front desk."

Paul was putting on a pair of sandals. He turned to his team. "Well, boys, I guess I'm out. No way I'm working for her. Who's coming with me?"

He pushed through the group and headed out toward the elevator. No one followed him. As the doors opened, he was greeted by a group of young women who rushed past him to greet Shania with hugs and high fives.

"This is the team that put up the GUST site," she explained. They started with nothing and built an architecture that can handle five times the traffic that our current site can manage."

Skip nodded. GUST was a new media darling, with news aggregated specifically for women 20-35, a demographic Pyramid would kill for. "So, this is the famous GUST Group. Now I know why you asked us to acquire them."

One of the members, who had bright blue hair, shook Skip's hand. "Amy Hull, chief officer."

"Glad to have you on board," Skip told her.

Amy gave Skip a side-eye. "Did you really buy us just because Shania told you to?"

Skip looked over. "Yep. Hey, she's my second favorite McCormack. And I trust her."

Joseph nodded. Skip had gotten the message.

Now the only question was … had the consumers? Only the next earnings report would tell.

Chapter Eighteen

Skip paused as his eyes took in the assembled forces on either side of the large table in the Florentine Room. Had it really been six months? In some ways, it had felt like six years, slogging through store after store, wading through profit and loss statements from markets as diverse as Portland, Oregon; Portland, Maine; and Portland, Arkansas. But in other ways, it felt like six days since he'd come before the McCormack family and asked them to trust him with their family legacy.

And there they were, the pro-Skip faction, led by Jenna and Shania on one side, and the old guard, with Gregor, Roberta, and Rockwell—with Rand Swigert clinging to him like a limpet—on the other. Many of the other family members had been leafing through the issue of *Business Insider* that Joseph's team had made sure to leave at every table setting.

This cover story was quite different from the one in *Forbes*. No blind quotes, no innuendo. Lots of positives about how the new, young CEO had regained the trust of his employees and their suppliers, and it even said that customers were "flocking back" to shop at their once-favorite family store. There was even a quote from a certain Booth Business School Professor named

Joseph Chandler. But as nice as it all was, today was the day it could all come to an end.

Letitia tapped her glass. "Ladies and gentlemen, please come to order," she sang out. "We have all enjoyed our luncheon. And now to the matters at hand." She turned to her left. "I believe Rockwell has something to say to start our meeting."

Rockwell was sitting, Buddha-like, with his hands folded across his expansive middle. He carefully stood up and bowed to his aunt. "Thank you, Aunt Letitia. Yes, I did ask to speak to you all before we hear from our young steward. Firstly, I think we all want to thank him for all the hard work he and his team have put in over the last six months."

Joseph looked over the table. It was possible to discern who was in Skip's camp by the enthusiasm with which they applauded this sentiment.

"I will be the first to admit that I doubted his vision and, even more, the ability to pull it off," Rockwell continued, with a genial smile. "How wrong I was!"

Skip turned to Joseph. "I don't like this. He's being too nice."

Rockwell gave a theatrical sigh. "But he also made us a promise, in this very room. He said he would vacate the position if we did not show a profit after those six months. And as of last month, we were still very much in the red."

He nodded to Rand, who stood up and began reading from a sheet of paper. "He projected an increase in store/site traffic, sales per square feet, inventory turns, which he promised would increase earnings by 5%, but sadly he did not make this number."

Skip bit his lip and then whispered to Joseph. "He's sharing only the data that show negative results and is ignoring KPIs that show positive momentum in the business."

"Let them make their pitch, and then you make yours,"

Joseph counseled. "I know it's hard to sit through this, but let's just see where things land after their ambush."

Gregor had joined his two associates and stood up. "I would like the record to show that a majority of McCormacks do not support the giveaways to the unions that were undertaken under this CEO's watch."

There were murmurs.

Shania coolly regarded her cousin with contempt. "And I would like the record to show that the majority of McCormacks who indeed have souls believe that the people who work for us deserve a living wage."

"Why you little…" Gregor sputtered.

Letitia tapped her glass so hard Skip thought it would break. "Children, please! No fighting! Let us be civil!"

"Aunt Letty is correct," Rockwell said. "There is no need for name-calling and hot tempers. We all want the same thing—for our family business to thrive."

"Do you want to compare earnings from when you were CEO to what they are under Mr. Collinsworth?" asked Audra McCormack. She was the daughter of Roberta who had sat meekly at the last meeting until she corrected her mother. It seems she'd found her voice.

Rockwell's eyes narrowed. "Times were different then, *dear* cousin. We were undergoing record inflation, and unemployment levels were skyrocketing."

"Excuses, excuses," muttered Audra.

Letitia stood. "I will not have this incivility at our board meeting. We are all one family and should treat one another with respect."

Roberta glared at her daughter. "What do you say to your Great Aunt?"

"I'm sorry, Great Aunt Letty," Audra said. "I just feel that it would be a shame if we gave Skip, here, the boot just when things are turning around."

Rand gave her what he thought was a fatherly look but it was more of a smirk. "Here's the thing, Ms. McCormack. We can't assess the long-term health of Pyramid based on one or two quarters of growth."

"But that's exactly what you *are* doing," Audra protested. "Essentially, you've said if Skip hasn't been able to turn a profit in two quarters, after years of plummeting sales and declining stock values when you were in charge, we should just give the reins back to you."

"Oh, I was *never* in charge," Rand said, turning to the room at large. "I was merely the chief financial officer. But if I do get a chance to run this once-great American company, I promise you it will be a very different story. I certainly wouldn't have spent $100 million on some paint and then turned our online presence over to a total neophyte with a team best known for posting kooky images of cats in pajamas, or whatever."

"No offense taken," Shania said. "And we've managed to take the mess your son's roommate made and turned it into one of Pyramid's biggest growth engines."

Rockwell gestured for Rand to sit down. Clearly, he'd done enough damage to their cause. "I ask that we hear from the man himself. He made a promise, and I would like to know if he intends to keep it," said Rockwell.

All eyes turned to Skip. He took a long sip of water and stood up. "Thank you, Rockwell. As you say, we are all in agreement that we want to save Pyramid, that is the goal. We simply don't agree on how to get there. I asked you to trust me for six months, and you did. I then brought that message of trust to our workers, our suppliers, and our customers—and it seems to be resonating."

"But the bottom line says it hasn't been enough," interjected Rockwell. "So, the question is, do you intend to keep your promise and step down, or shall I call for a vote of no confidence?"

Skip took a moment. "I, of course, am a man of my word and I will do what I said. But now is not the time to disrupt the business. With the momentum we're building, we have clear visibility at both topline and bottom-line growth."

"How much time, Skip? "Rockwell demanded. "Six more months? Another $100 million? Are you asking, once again, to throw good money after bad?"

"There is such a thing as cutting our losses," Roberta added. "You know I had a wonderful chef. But the man drank. He made an amazing *boeuf bourguignon,* but I still had to let him go. It broke my heart, but I just couldn't trust him once I knew he couldn't hold his liquor."

The room fell silent.

"Mother, what does *that* have to do with anything?" asked Audra.

"Just because someone is doing a good job now doesn't mean they won't mess up in the future, isn't that what you were getting at?" suggested Rand.

"My point exactly!" Roberta said, happily.

Rockwell eyed Skip. "Very well. So, you are forcing a vote? Even after not fulfilling the terms of our agreement?"

"I guess that's what we should do," Jenna interjected. "Rand only shared negative news with us. He ignored KPIs that show strong positive momentum, some of them for the first time in over twenty years. Skip has done his best."

"And it wasn't good enough," said Rockwell. "I call for a vote."

Letitia sighed. "Very well. A vote has been called for, so all in favor of—

"Wait!" Joseph's voice was loud and commanding.

Letitia peered over at him. "I'm sorry, sir, but this is a family matter."

Joseph held up his phone. "This has just come out in *The Wall Street Journal* live feed. It's a leak of Pyramid store's next quarterly income statement."

Rockwell whirled and turned on Rand. "How did this happen?"

Rand looked like he was in shock. "It was secure. There was no way anyone could have seen those numbers unless we were hacked."

Jenna turned to Shania who was looking very pleased with herself. "Shania, was it?"

Shania grinned. "I'll never tell. But it's amazing what you can do with computers these days, huh?"

Joseph tried his best to keep his voice calm but there still was a slight tremble. This wasn't some classroom case study. This had been a part of his life for six months. He read off the screen. "Based on confidential data acquired by this publication, Pyramid, the struggling retail giant, seems to have turned the corner at last. It grew revenue at high single digits and delivered strong profits in its third quarter. The turnaround by its new CEO, Skip Collingsworth, seems to be taking hold. Could this be the beginning of the next generation of growth for Pyramid?"

Leticia stood and began clapping. Even Roberta and Gregor joined in, applauding enthusiastically.

Jenna turned to Joseph and whispered, "Any time something happens that can make the McCormacks more money, they're all for it!"

Skip called out to Rockwell. "I'm sorry, you were saying. Do you still wish to call a vote?"

Rockwell's face reddened and he wiped the perspiration off his forehead with a napkin. He turned unsteadily to Rand, who was busy checking his phone. "Under the circumstances, I believe a postponement is in order," he muttered before he was drowned out by the celebration around him.

Many of the McCormacks surrounded Skip, patting him on the back and assuring him that they'd trusted him all along.

Chapter Nineteen

Joseph checked his watch for the hundredth time.

"You do that one more time and I swear I'll slap you," warned Dionne. "You know he'll be here. He said he would."

Joseph nodded. "I know. It's just that he's a pretty busy guy these days." He nervously paced around the area by the store's front door.

"Like you're not?" she said. She looked into the parking lot and watched as a black Lincoln Town Car pulled in. "See? I told you. Right on time. You need to listen to your wife."

The door opened and Skip and Jenna stepped out, waving. Jenna walked over and kissed Joseph on the cheek. Then Skip wrapped his arms around him for a full-on hug.

"Here's the man! I missed you, guy!" Skip shouted.

Before Joseph could say anything, Jenna had turned to his wife. "You must be the famous Dionne!" she exclaimed.

"The power behind the throne," Dionne said dryly.

The two women exchanged hugs.

"Shall we?" proposed Joseph, gesturing to the entrance behind him.

There, gleaming in the summer sunlight, was the Pyramid

Store where thirty years earlier, fourteen-year-old Joseph Chandler had bought school clothes and shoes that would take him to his new life, and onto the path that led him to Skip and the adventure of the last six months. It felt right that they were able to walk in together.

The two couples made their way through the spotless glass doors, where they were immediately greeted by an older woman in a clean blue vest inside the store.

"Good morning!" she called out. "Can I help you lovely people find anything?"

"We're fine," said Joseph. "Just looking around."

The woman beamed. "You take your time, honey. I bet you'll find something. Do you have children?"

"Two boys," said Dionne.

"We've got the newest Lego sets in the toys section, aisle A15," the woman told her with a wink.

Joseph smiled. "We'll keep that in mind."

As they walked through, Skip turned to Joseph. "Did you hear that? She knew her inventory and where to send us. We're doing something right, I guess!"

"So, it would seem," Joseph said.

As they made their way through the store, more sales associates asked if they needed help with their shopping. Somehow, word had gotten around that the CEO was in the store, and the manager ran up to greet them. She was a small, nervous-looking woman. "Mr. Collinsworth! What a surprise to see you here! Is everything all right?"

"Everything is absolutely wonderful, Mrs. Pam Geiger, is it?" said Skip reading her nametag.

"None of my people are on their phones, are they?" she asked. "We have pretty strict rules about that. That's what the break is for."

Joseph shook his head. "Nope. Everyone seems to be focused on their customers. And there seem to be a lot of them."

Pam looked down and smiled shyly. "We're doing our best. And it's wonderful to be this busy." She leaned in. "I've been at Pyramid since the old days, so I'm especially grateful."

Jenna needed to buy something for a baby shower, so she and Dionne wandered over to the well-marked area for children's clothes and accessories.

Skip took in the busy jangle of carts and the noise of giggling kids and teenagers trying out the newest tech in the electronics department. "Music to my ears," he said happily.

"Mr. Chandler? Joseph Chandler?"

Joseph turned to see Josie Kirkland, the woman he'd first interviewed all those months ago. She was trailed by her kids, John Lewis, and Marion Anderson.

"Well, I didn't expect to see you here!" Josie declared. "Don't tell me you're a Pyramid customer?"

"I am today," Joseph laughed. "Skip, this is Josie Kirkland. She's one of the people who helped us figure out what was wrong with Pyramid. Josie, this is the man who runs all of Pyramid."

"Well, you are doing one heck of a good job, if I may say so," she said and patted Skip on the shoulder. "I swore I'd never come back into this store again. But after all my friends started telling me about the bargains they were getting here I had to come to see for myself. Besides, these two need new bathing suits. And it's such a nice place now!"

"Very nice to meet you, Mrs. Kirkland," Skip said as she checked her list and moved on.

"Don't look now, Skip, but I believe our wives are stuck behind that giant panda," Joseph told him.

Dionne was holding one arm of the huge stuffed animal as Jenna carried the rest.

"You're not seriously giving that to Carrie are you?" Skip asked.

"Of course, we are," Jenna's voice came from behind the bear. "It will look darling in her nursery."

Joseph and Skip guided her to the escalator down to the first floor, where they headed to the cashiers. Skip noted that the self-service registers were filled with people checking out, but just as many people seemed to like the human contact with the workers who manned the cash registers. They headed over to one with a short line and soon were paying.

A middle-aged Indian woman with the name tag "Chhaya" greeted them. "Hello and thank you for shopping at Pyramid. Did you find everything you were looking for?"

Skip glanced at the huge bear. "Everything and more, I should say."

Chhaya took his card and noticed the name. "You are the man who changed everything, aren't you?" she asked shyly.

"Well, I had a lot of help," answered Skip. "Especially from this guy."

"It has been so wonderful. I remember months ago complaining to that nice young man who came to talk to me and my husband about the store."

Joseph thought for a moment. "Your husband?"

She pointed to a man in a security guard uniform by one of the doors. "That is he, Darpan. The young man was so nice, telling our children tales from the Mahabharata."

Joseph smiled. "Do you remember his name, by any chance?"

Chhaya's face lit up. "Of course. His name was Samesh

Bhati. He came from a town just like the one where Darpan and I grew up."

"Well, isn't that a coincidence!" exclaimed Joseph. "He happens to be a good friend of mine. I'll tell him you said hello!"

"Please do that," Chhaya said, as she gave Skip back his card. "I hope he is well."

Joseph thought of his young colleagues. "Yes, I think he is doing quite well, as a matter of fact."

Epilogue

A few days later, as students throughout the campus were clearing out their dorm rooms, there was a knock on the door of Joseph Chandler's office.

Joseph called out, "Come in!" Then quickly got up to greet Gabby and Sam.

"Congratulations on Pyramid, Professor Chandler," Sam said.

"I think that I should be the one congratulating you two," Joseph replied. "After all, it isn't every day that I get a newly minted MBA *and* a brand new PhD in my office at the same time!"

Gabby slung herself over the chair facing Joseph's desk. "So, you wanted to see us?"

"I was curious about your future," Joseph said, as he headed back behind his desk.

Sam had taken the seat next to Gabby and they exchanged glances. Sam spoke first. "To be honest, this has been quite a subject of discussion."

Gabby reached out and took Sam's hand. "We're kind of up in the air. Sam is looking for jobs at universities where he can pursue his research and hopefully teach. I don't know, I might want to teach, too. But I also liked being in the outside world with you, solving actual problems instead of theoretical ones."

Joseph turned to Sam. "What about you?"

Sam's face was glowing. "Oh, yes! It was very exhilarating, and also wonderful to make people's lives better. To make them see how the wisdom of ancient texts can still be relevant."

"I'm glad to hear that," Joseph said. "And here's why." He motioned to a pile of papers on the right corner of his desk. "You see that? Those are offers for consulting gigs. I mean, dozens. They came in once the news of my involvement in helping transform the fortunes of Pyramid Stores came out."

"That's fantastic!" exclaimed Gabby. "You deserve it."

"Here's the thing," Joseph continued. "I wouldn't have gotten these offers without the two of you."

Sam and Gabby exchanged glances. Sam finally spoke. "Professor, are you suggesting—"

"Yes, I'm asking you two to come aboard with me to start a consulting firm. This way I can continue teaching, you can work on your translations, and Gabby can polish that silver medal that I can finally congratulate her on winning."

Gabby nodded. "Okay, okay. Very funny. But let's say we do join you. How would it work?"

"Well, it's been working just fine as it is," Joseph said. "If you mean financially, we'll split the fee three ways to make it fair."

The three sat for a moment.

"I think the answer is yes," Sam said slowly, looking over at Gabby, who nodded.

Joseph crossed his arms and sat back, looking satisfied. "So, there are only two questions left. First, what shall we call ourselves?"

"CRB Consulting?" suggested Gabby.

"A little generic, don't you think?" answered Joseph. "We need something special—something memorable."

Sam thought for a moment. "Trikaya."

Gabby tried it out. "Trikaya. I like it."

"I do, too," Joseph said. "What does it mean?"

Sam smiled. "It is a Sanskrit word meaning 'three bodies.'"

"Perfect! Trikaya Consulting it is!" Joseph declared.

Gabby looked confused. "Okay, that's the first question. What's the other one?"

Joseph grinned and turned to his right where the pile of offers sat, beckoning them with promises of more troubled companies, more challenges, and more puzzles to be solved.

"Well, boys and girls, which case do we take on next?"

A Note to the Reader

While the story that you just read is a fable, and there is no such firm as Trikaya, the issues presented in the story are extremely real. The most valuable possession of a company is not its trademarks or patents—it's trust. It doesn't matter how long your company has been in business, what last year's balance sheet looks like, what the stock price is, or even what people say about you on social media. What matters is the level of trust that you command in the marketplace.

This is a story about a once-trusted company that lost its way. The challenge with traditional consulting approaches, as we discuss in the book, is that they are primarily tactical. They pick off important issues, to be sure, but they do not resolve the main problem that enterprises often face today: Do we enjoy trust in the marketplace? Because without trust, there is nothing.

Astute readers will examine the process by which Pyramid chose to go forward with its focus on building trust. They will recognize that CEOs don't make decisions of this magnitude after a meeting with some well-meaning, if slightly amateurish, consultants. Instead, there would be enormous amounts of research done, at all levels of the company. The CEO would need to achieve buy-in from executives up and down the line. While you and I both know that's a fact of business life, I omitted much of that process for the sake of keeping the story moving forward.

I came to the United States from India, which gives me an invaluable perspective on business and on life. In India, because our culture is ancient, we take the long view. In over three decades here, helping companies shape the future and drive billions of equity value growth, I have relied on a framework I built. It incorporates three elements represented in the consultancy established in this story—a framework grounded on proven social and behavioral science principles, ancient wisdom, and actionable modern-day management principles.

I hope you enjoyed meeting Joseph, Gabby, and Sam. Now that their firm has been established, you can expect to find them solving other major, relatable business issues in future books! I hope you enjoyed *The Pyramid Puzzle*, and I look forward to sharing more adventures of their newly hatched consulting firm in the near future.

About the Author

ZAIN RAJ is a bestselling author of *BRAND RITUALS™: How Successful Brands Bond with Customers for Life* and *MARKETING FOR TOMORROW, NOT YESTERDAY: Surviving and Thriving in the Insight Economy™*. Zain has spent over three and a half decades helping grow some of the most compelling companies on the planet. A futurist, inventor, and agitator, his deep understanding of human behavior, ability to predict the future, disruptive thinking, and future-forward insights have helped create over $100 billion in equity value for multiple corporations just in the past decade. Zain is an evangelist for innovation and a strong believer in empowering others. He is a much sought-after speaker, teacher, advisor, and contributor to leading publications, media channels, universities, and conferences.

THE NEXT BOOK IN THIS SERIES:

I hope you enjoyed this story and enjoyed meeting and getting to know Skip, Joseph, Gabby, Sam, and all the protagonists and antagonists in ***THE PYRAMID PUZZLE***. I truly enjoyed bringing them and their experiences to life.

Here's a question for you... Would you like to read about other problems the Trikaya team of Joseph, Gabby, and Sam take on next?

Well... our terrific trio has agreed to take on a challenge to help future-proof a company whose business model was destroyed by the pandemic. It is a fun adventure involving a talented heiress, flying cars, machine learning, artificial intelligence, and a colorful cast of characters, which together make the story real, interesting, and educational.

If you would like to get this story before we release it across all platforms, you can preorder it on the Kindle app, Amazon.com, or at zainraj.com. Be the first to read it and join Trikaya's next adventure.

A PERSONAL REQUEST:

If you enjoyed THE PYRAMID PUZZLE, I would appreciate it if you could leave an unbiased review on Amazon/Kindle, Audible, and Goodreads to help others who might enjoy and benefit from this story.

MY SOCIAL COORDINATES:

If you would like to know more about me/follow my interests and perspectives:

Visit me at zainraj.com.
LinkedIn at https://www.linkedin.com/in/zainrajinfluencer/
Facebook at https://www.facebook.com/zainrajmarketer/
Instagram at @rajzainul

A COUPLE OF BOOKS YOU SHOULD READ:

Based on my study and practice of human behavior, I developed an approach that creates deep emotional connections between brands and their consumers. The values, beliefs, and bonds that brands build with their consumers result in strong and lasting bonds. This was the subject of my first book, ***BRAND RITUALS™: How Successful Brands Bond with Customers for Life***—widely regarded as a seminal work in this area and used by universities to teach brand development principles. It was the #1 marketing and sales bestseller on Amazon.

My second book (also a bestseller) is based on an exploration of emerging technologies that are shaping the future of business and marketing. In this book, I framed the definition of a 'Decathlete Marketeer™' and formulated the construct for businesses to win in a continually reshaping world, disrupted by innovation, empowered by technology, but most importantly, inspired by human creativity and empathy. I called this world, the 'Insight Economy™' in the book titled, ***MARKETING FOR TOMORROW, NOT YESTERDAY: Surviving and Thriving in the Insight Economy™*** that provides practical insights on the principles businesses and brands should use to not just adapt but challenge in today's continually reshaping landscape.

www.ingramcontent.com/pod-product-compliance
Lightning Source LLC
Chambersburg PA
CBHW070404200726
48294CB00003B/1084
* 9 7 8 1 9 6 0 2 9 9 0 7 9 *